PAPERIE

PAPERIE

100 CREATIVE PAPERCRAFT IDEAS

GIFTS • DÉCOR • STATIONERY • ACCESSORIES

KIRSTY NEALE

D&C

David and Charles

CONTENTS

INTRODUCTION

As a material, paper is familiar to everyone. Thanks to technology, we may use it rather less than we once did, but it's still part of most people's everyday life. From fragile tissue to thick, strong cardboard, plain white copier paper to highly patterned gift wrap, it's as varied in texture and type as it is versatile in application. But, while there's every chance you've already used it creatively in some way (who hasn't folded and thrown a paper plane across their desk?), you may have less than positive preconceptions about the idea of papercrafting.

This book sets out to show you it's not only possible, but also simple to create beautiful, contemporary projects from paper. Using it as both a material and, in some cases, a tool, the projects cover a range of techniques, including origami, collage, papercutting and papier mâché. Many projects can be completed with everyday types of paper, such as gift wrap or scraps of wallpaper, while others offer the perfect opportunity to recycle or re-purpose materials like old maps, books and security envelopes.

At the back of the book, you'll find some instant projects – ideas you can cut out and make straight away, plus a selection of patterned papers to use elsewhere. Some of the pages are double-sided, so you can make the project and then use the patterned side of the leftover scraps, *or* photocopy the sheet and use both sides in full.

Whatever your level of skill and experience, the ideas throughout can be adapted to suit your taste, requirements and the paper supplies you have to hand. Use them as inspiration, not just instruction, and enjoy creating beautiful projects for yourself, your family, your friends and your home.

VISUAL INDEX

The projects in the book are divided across ten categories. Each category has its own icon and these are noted on the project page, as well as in this useful Visual Index. In order to quickly identify what you want to make, just find the relevant icon in the Visual Index. For instance, if you're looking for something that

would work well as a gift, simply find the Gift Ideas icon in the Index, and read through the list to find a suitable project.

Don't let the Index constrain you; if you want to give a piece of jewellery from the Wearable category as a gift, or use a decoration from Parties + Weddings as a fun piece of home décor, go ahead and do it!

Stationery

Cards + Wrapping

Wearable

(Including jewellery)

Re-used + Recycled

At Home

Fun Stuff

On the Wall

(Including pictures and
simple art pieces)

Gift Ideas

Parties
+ Weddings

Instant Fix

(Projects made using the cut-out
sheets at the back of the book)

MATERIALS + EQUIPMENT

You can start making paper-based projects with the most basic of supplies – plain paper, scissors and maybe a pen or pencil – but these are some extras you might also find useful.

Equipment

- **Craft knife** – find one that's comfortable to hold, and keep a good supply of fresh blades on hand, too.
- **Self-healing cutting mat** – buy the largest you can afford and you can then use it for projects of any size.
- **Steel ruler** – don't try to use a plastic or wooden ruler when cutting with a craft knife.
- **Scissors** – you'll need a large, general-purpose pair, plus a small, sharp pair for cutting fine details.
- **Hole punch** – a standard office punch will often do, but for more versatility, e.g., cutting through thick card, try a Crop-a-dile (this also works as a useful eyelet-setting tool).
- **Paper punches** – you're likely to use simple, adaptable shapes the most, so start off with circles, squares, flowers and a heart.
- **Corner rounder** – these give a smart, alternative finish to cards. If you like the look, buy an inexpensive, punch-style version or something stronger, like a Corner Chomper.
- **Disposable nail file or fine sandpaper** – for smoothing edges, joins and papier mâché pieces.

- **Brayer** – an optional tool for flattening layers and strengthening adhesion over large surfaces. (You can sometimes use an old rolling pin instead.)
- **Piercing tool** – used to pierce holes in paper. A large, sharp needle will often work instead.
- **Sewing machine or needle and thread** – it's almost always possible to adapt a machine-stitched project to one that can be sewn by hand if you don't have a machine.
- **Computer and printer** – these are optional but useful tools for printing out text, patterned paper, templates and so on.
- **Small paintbrushes** – for detailed worked on projects.
- **Craft foam or old mouse mat** – use as a surface when piercing holes in paper.
- **Embossing stylus** – you may be able to use a dried-out ballpoint pen for some projects as an alternative.
- **Stamps** – see Techniques: Stamping and Embossing for types.

Paper

- **Patterned paper** – use gift wrap, scrapbooking paper, origami paper and so on, or try printing sheets at home, either from pattern sourcebooks or digital files sold online.
- **Recycled or upcycled papers** – for instance, old/unwanted magazines, books, catalogues, maps, stamps, postcards, leaflets, packaging, security envelopes or notebook pages (lined, squared, graph, manuscript, and so on).
- **Tissue paper** – plain and patterned sheets.
- **Thin card** – white and coloured, also pre-folded card blanks for making greetings cards.
- **Thick/strong card** – this is sometimes known as chipboard. You can recycle pieces from board-backed envelopes. Alternatively, it is sold in larger sheets as greyboard in art and craft shops.

- **Mountboard** – similar in weight and strength to greyboard, it has a clean, white core and comes in a wide range of ready-to-display colours. It's also found in art and craft shops.
- **Tracing paper** – useful for transferring patterns, or as a translucent, vellum-like design detail.
- **Corrugated card** – this can be recycled from large grocery or packing boxes.
- **Watercolour paper** – available in various weights, with thicker sheets being more like card than paper. Cold-press has a bumpy, textured surface, while hot-press is much smoother.
- **Grungeboard** – this is a very strong, flexible type of card, which is almost impossible to tear. It is usually only available to buy in very small sheets.

Other Materials

- **Adhesive** – most of the projects in the book will specify the best type of glue to use, whether it's a glue stick, PVA (also known as white or tacky glue), spray adhesive, double-sided tape or a clear, hard-drying glue, such as Glossy Accents.

- **Hot glue gun** – an instant-grab adhesive that bonds very quickly and is especially tough on porous surfaces, such as cardboard. Not essential, but useful.

- **Paint** – standard acrylic, plus spray paint for some projects.

- **Découpage medium** – spreadable matte or glossy adhesive, such as Mod Podge, or artist's gel medium. Mod Podge can also be used as an alternative to varnish over a finished project.

- **Wallpaper paste** – use for papier mâché projects, buy in powder form and mix as needed. The paste and unmixed powder can be stored in jars for long periods.

- **Fine nylon/beading thread** – useful for stringing banners, mobiles and so on. Much stronger than regular sewing thread, but just as fine, flexible and easy to use.

- **Permanent marker pens** – for adding details to projects.

- **Paper fasteners** – also known as brads, basic types can be found in stationery supply shops, or a variety of shapes, colours and sizes in craft ranges.

- **Varnish** – to seal and protect finish projects (optional). Use a paper-compatible artist's varnish in matte, glossy or satin finish, as preferred.

- **Paper clay** – air-drying modelling material made from paper fibres. Store in an airtight container, to prevent unused pieces drying out.

- **Washi or decorative tape** – for adding decoration to projects.

- **General embellishments** – items such as beads, buttons and sequins for decorating.

- **Picture frames** – either new or recycled, for framing finished art pieces.

- **Dowel sticks** – buy long lengths in craft/hobby shops or DIY stores, and cut to length with a craft knife or hacksaw.

- **Bamboo skewers** – similar to dowel, but usually thinner. Find them in supermarkets. Cut to size with strong scissors.

- **Inkpads and embossing powder** – see Techniques: Stamping and Embossing.

- **Ribbon, cord, string, twine** – for decorative tying and binding. Use new and/or recycled from presents and packaging.

- **Wooden clothespegs (clothespins)** – useful for holding pieces together as glue dries, and also as a simple, alternative way to display artwork.

- **Polystyrene shapes** – find poly-balls and other forms in good art and craft shops.

- **Paper drinking straws** – used as structural elements in some of the projects.

- **Wire** – various thickness and gauges are used (see note in Techniques: Jewellery).

- **Binder rings** – hinged metal rings, similar to those used inside ring-binder folders. Find in craft/hobby or stationery shops.

- **Basic jewellery-making supplies** – see Techniques: Jewellery.

- **Clear acetate** – flexible, transparent plastic, available in sheets from art shops or stationery stores.

THE PROJECTS

MAGNETIC PAPER QUILT

YOU WILL NEED:

Flat, metal baking sheet
Card
Patterned papers
PVA glue
Brayer or rolling pin
Clear varnish (optional)

TECHNIQUE: Découpage

TIP / Use this colourful idea to brighten up an office or kitchen, keeping day-to-day reminders close at hand.

1 Copy the hexagon template provided onto a piece of card and cut out. Draw around it onto a selection of patterned papers and cut out.

2 Spread a thin layer of glue over the back of your first hexagon, especially the edges. Place it in the centre of the baking sheet and press firmly into place. Roll a brayer or rolling pin over the top to make sure it's firmly adhered and flat.

3 Add a second hexagon next to the first one, lining up the edges so they fit together neatly. Keep going, building up a tessellated, quilt-style pattern of hexagons.

4 When you reach the edges of the baking sheet, carefully fold the paper pieces over onto the back. To negotiate curved corners (or if your tray has holes at the top), cut small slits in the paper, like sunrays radiating out from the edge of the tray. Fold over the sections between the slits to create a smooth corner without lumps or creasing.

5 Allow the glue to dry. Brush on an (optional) coat of clear varnish to seal and protect the tray.

PATTERNED CLIPBOARDS

YOU WILL NEED:

Plain (masonite) clipboard
Patterned paper
Spray adhesive or PVA glue

1 Take a piece of scrap paper and place it with one edge overlapping the mechanism at the top of the clipboard. Push the paper against the edges of the mechanism with the tip of your scissors, as if tracing around it, but marking an indent in the paper.

2 Cut along the indented line. Check the paper fits neatly around the mechanism and adjust if necessary before using the paper as a template.

3 Cut a piece of patterned paper slightly larger than the board. Trace the template onto the back of the patterned paper, close to the upper edge. Cut out and check it fits neatly around the mechanism.

4 Apply glue to the back of the patterned paper and press down firmly onto the front of the clipboard. Allow to dry, before trimming away excess paper from the edges. Hang your clipboard on the wall and use it as a simple 'frame' to clip up photos or pictures.

Alternative:

Paint a plain clipboard, or cover with plain paper (as above). Cut out a selection of patterned-paper shapes (e.g., hexagons) in different sizes. Glue each one to the front of the clipboard, building up a pattern of your choice.

TIP / If your finished notebook doesn't want to stay folded, you can fix the problem by placing it under something flat and heavy (e.g., a pile of heavy hardback books) for a few hours.

FOLD + STITCH DIY BOOKS

YOU WILL NEED:

Sheets of paper (e.g., plain sketch paper, lined sheets or pages from an old ledger)
Thin card (plain or patterned)
Sewing machine or needle and thread
Label

TECHNIQUE: Sewing on Paper

1 Cut the paper into pieces, 12 x 19cm (4¾ x 7½in). You can adjust this to create a larger or smaller book. Depending on the thickness of each sheet, aim to cut out 12–20 pieces.

2 To make the cover, cut a 12.5 x 19.5cm (5 x 7¾in) rectangle of thin card. Fold the card cover and the paper pages in half.

3 Gather the pages together in a bundle, lining up the edges and the centre folds. Place the cover at the bottom of the pile, making sure there's an even amount of card overhanging the pages at the top and bottom edges.

4 Stitch along the centre fold, sewing through all layers, by hand or machine.

5 Pull the thread ends through to the inside of the book and knot together. Snip off any excess thread, and then add a strip of washi tape along the stitched centre fold to neaten and hold the knotted ends in place.

6 Fold the book firmly in half, and add a label to the front cover. You can use your own or one of the labels provided on the cut-out sheet.

PAPER BEAD PENDANTS

YOU WILL NEED:

Thin paper (e.g., pages recycled from a fashion or interiors magazine/ catalogue, or leftover gift wrap)

Scrap of card

PVA glue

Cocktail stick

Clear varnish

Jewellery wire (26-gauge)

Chain

Pliers

1 Copy the bead template provided onto patterned paper and cut out. Spread a thin layer of glue over the back of the paper, as marked on the template.

2 Starting at the narrow end, roll the shape around a cocktail stick. Press the wider end down firmly to secure.

3 Make five or six beads in the same way. Allow to dry and then brush on two coats of clear varnish.

4 Cut a 30cm (12in) length of jewellery wire and slide a paper bead along to the centre. Take another bead and thread one end of the wire through the centre from left to right. Thread the other end through from right to left. Gently pull both wire ends so the bead slides down and sits on top of the first one. Add the rest of the beads in the same way.

5 Use pliers to cut a 70–90cm (27½– 35½in) length of chain. Thread the wire at one side of the beads through the link at one end of the chain. Twist gently but firmly to secure. Repeat to join the opposite end of the chain to the opposite side of the beads.

6 Snip off the wire ends, leaving a 3cm (1¼in) tail. Tuck this back inside the top bead, and add a blob of glue at each end to stop the wire tails slipping out.

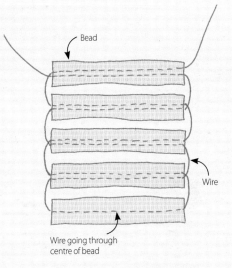

Bead

Wire

Wire going through centre of bead

TIP/ For a different look, thread your beads onto a leather thong (real or faux) instead. Adjust the size of the template to make larger beads and mix in some round wooden beads, too.

INSTAGRAM PHOTO ALBUM

1 Cut four pieces of cardboard, as shown in the diagram. Glue patterned paper to one side of pieces A and D, folding a 2cm (¾in) wide border over to the back on all sides.

YOU WILL NEED:

Thick card
Glue stick
Patterned paper (2–3 contrasting prints)
Self-adhesive vinyl/sticky-backed plastic
Single-hole punch (e.g., a Crop-a-dile)
Graph paper
Wooden coffee stirrer
Washi tape
Rubber band
Label

TECHNIQUE: Folding + Scoring

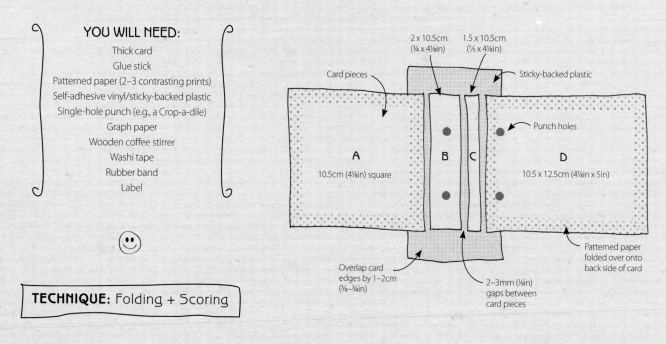

2 x 10.5cm (¾ x 4⅛in)
1.5 x 10.5cm (⅝ x 4⅛in)
Card pieces
Sticky-backed plastic
Punch holes

A
10.5cm (4⅛in) square

B C

D
10.5 x 12.5cm (4⅛in x 5in)

Overlap card edges by 1–2cm (⅜–¾in)

2–3mm (⅛in) gaps between card pieces

Patterned paper folded over onto back side of card

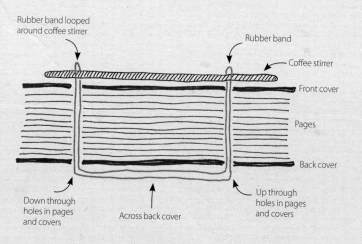

Rubber band looped around coffee stirrer

Rubber band

Coffee stirrer

Front cover

Pages

Back cover

Down through holes in pages and covers

Across back cover

Up through holes in pages and covers

2 Cut a 6 x 14.5cm (2⅜ x 5¼in) strip of adhesive vinyl. Place the card pieces on top (as shown in diagram). Fold the excess vinyl over to the back.

3 Glue a 10cm (4in) square of contrasting paper to the back of piece A, and a 10 x 12cm (4 x 4¾in) rectangle to piece D. Add a 6 x 10cm (2⅜ x 4in) strip of adhesive vinyl to the centre back, lining up the side edges with the piece folded over from the front. Punch holes either side of the spine, as marked on the diagram.

4 Cut 24 pieces of graph paper, each 10 x 12cm (4 x 4¾in). Glue together back to back in pairs, and fold over 2cm (¾in) at the left-hand edges. Punch holes in the folded sections, lining them up with the holes in the cover. Cut the ends off the coffee stirrer, so it's 9cm (3½in) long and cover with decorative tape.

5 Place the pages inside the cover. Loop the rubber band around the coffee stirrer, then take it down through the top hole in the front cover and each of the pages. Go out through the top hole in the back cover, then back up through the lower hole in the back cover, the pages and front cover. Loop it around the opposite end of the coffee stirrer to hold in place.

6 Add a label and a title or logo to the cover. Fix your photographs into place using strips of washi tape.

TIP / You can easily add extra pages later on by removing and then re-threading the rubber band.

CHEVRON GARLAND

TECHNIQUE: Sewing on Paper

1 Copy the chevron template onto scrap card and cut out. Trace around it twice onto plain or patterned paper and cut the pieces out. Glue them together, back to back.

2 Repeat, to make as many double-layered chevrons as desired, using a mixture of different papers. Allow the glue to dry for at least an hour.

3 Pull out a long length of thread (both bobbin and top threads) from your sewing machine, to make it easier to hang your garland. Place the edge of your first chevron under the sewing foot and feed it through the machine, stitching along the middle from top to bottom. When you reach the bottom, make a few extra stitches with nothing under the foot and then add your second chevron. Stitch along the centre, as you did before.

4 Keep going, adding one chevron at a time, and leaving a small length of thread between each one.

5 When you're happy with the garland's length, stop stitching and pull out another long length of thread as you did at the start. Snip the ends to release.

 TIP Hang the finished garland vertically or horizontally. Display several together with the chevrons pointing in alternate directions for a bolder effect.

PAPER BOW GARLAND

YOU WILL NEED:

Patterned papers
Glue stick
Nylon beading thread or fine string
Needle
Washi tape

TIP / Make single bows following steps 1–3 and use them to decorate wrapped gifts.

1 Copy the bow templates onto paper, using one pattern for the bow itself and a contrasting print for the tails and centre strip. Cut out all pieces.

2 Fold one end of the bow piece over and glue to the centre back. Do the same with the opposite end. This forms the bow shape, with a loop at either end.

3 Stick the tail strip to the back of the bow. Wrap the centre strip around both pieces and stick the overlapped ends together. Make more bows in the same way (the total number depends on how long you want the finished garland to be, but aim for at least six).

4 Cut a length of thread and use a needle to feed it through the centre strip at the back of your first bow. Slide the bow along the thread. Add the rest in the same way.

5 Position the bows along the length of the thread, spacing them out evenly. Turn them over, one at a time, and tape the string to the back of the tail strip on each side. This will hold the bows in place and help the garland to drape properly.

WINDMILL STRAWS + PAPER PICKS

YOU WILL NEED:

Paper and/or thin card
Needle and thread
Small button
Drinking straws
Decorative tape
Glue stick
Heart and butterfly punches (optional)
Cocktail sticks

☆

TECHNIQUE: Folding + Scoring

To make the windmill straws:

1 Cut a 6cm (2⅜in) square of paper and fold in half diagonally. Press along the fold to create a neat crease, then smooth the paper out. Repeat along the opposite diagonal.

2 Cut along the creased lines, starting at each corner and stopping 1cm (⅜in) from the centre of the square. Use a needle to make a hole at each corner and two in the centre (see diagram).

3 Thread the needle, tie a temporary knot in the end of your thread and bring it up through one of the centre holes. Working from front to back each time, push the needle through each of the four corner holes in turn, so they pull in towards the centre.

4 Thread the needle up through one of the holes in a button and down through the other. Now go back down through the four corner holes, following your original thread.

5 Go down through the second centre hole in the paper and pull the thread ends taut to form the finished windmill.

6 Position the windmill over the front of a straw, and knot the thread ends together at the back to hold in place. Snip off the excess thread.

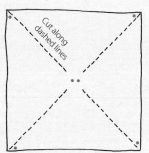

Make holes where marked by dots

TIP / For extra impact, the folded windmills can be constructed from double-sided paper. Choose prints that are different in colour and style for the best effect, such as the lime dots and black and white striped version shown.

To make the heart picks:

Punch or cut out two hearts from thin card. Stick them together, back-to-back, with the top of a cocktail stick sandwiched between.

To make the banner picks:

Cut a strip of paper, spread glue over the back and fold it in half around the top of a cocktail stick. Press the ends together firmly, before cutting them into a neat V shape.

To make the butterfly picks:

Punch or cut out four symmetrical butterflies. Fold them in half vertically. Spread glue over the left side of one butterfly and stick to the right side of a second. Spread glue over the left side of the second butterfly and stick to the right side of a third. Add some glue to the top of a cocktail stick and place between the three butterflies. Spread glue over the back of the last butterfly and press onto the backs of the first and third butterflies, so the cocktail stick is sandwiched in the centre.

TIP / Use any leftover flowers to decorate a gift-wrapped parcel or simple card.

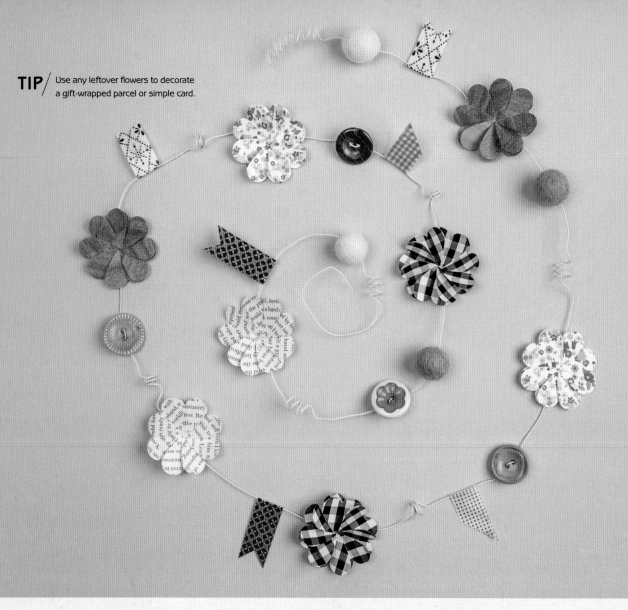

PAPER + WIRE GARLAND

YOU WILL NEED:

Plain or patterned paper
Heart and circle punches (optional)
Glue stick
Jewellery wire (approx. 22-gauge)
Scissors or pliers
Pencil or knitting needle
Buttons and/or felt balls
Washi tape

1 To make a flower, punch or cut out eight symmetrical hearts from paper. Fold each one in half vertically. Cut a circle of thin card, roughly the same height as the hearts.

2 Apply glue to the back of a heart, on the right-hand side of the fold line only. Stick the heart to the card circle, with the pointed end roughly in the centre of the circle.

3 Apply glue to a second heart in the same way. Stick it to the card circle, lining up the centre fold with the stuck-down edge of the first heart.

4 Keep going, adding each of the hearts in turn. The right-hand edge of the last one should neatly line up with the fold in the first heart.

5 Cut a length of wire 50cm (20in) longer than the desired length of your finished garland. Starting 10–15cm (4–6in) from one end, wrap the wire around a pencil several times to create a spiral. Thread on a button or felt ball.

6 Fold a piece of tape over the wire and snip a V shape in the end to make a flag. Cut an extra card circle and cover one side with glue. Place a paper flower against the wire and press the circle over the back to hold in place. Add more flowers, flags, buttons, felt balls and spiral twists along the length of the wire.

MOBILE PHONE CASE

YOU WILL NEED:

Thin card or paper (colours for hair and
skin, plus patterned pieces)
Pale pink tissue
Clear plastic mobile phone case/cover
Fine black marker pen
Craft knife
Clear-drying adhesive

TECHNIQUE: Collage

1 Copy the head and body template onto flesh-toned card
and cut out. Draw on facial features. Stick two small circles
of pink tissue to the lower edge of the face and trim excess.
Copy the clothing templates onto patterned paper, cut out
and glue to the bottom of the body.

2 Trace around the edges of the phone case onto paper in
your chosen hair colour. Cut out, snipping just inside the
traced lines, then cut a smaller area out to allow for your
phone's camera lens. Slot into the case to check it fits and trim
to make any adjustments.

3 Use a fine black marker to draw vertical lines over one side
of the paper. With a craft knife, cut a slit across the paper,
slightly wider than the face and about a third of the way
down from the top. Slide the top of the face through the slit,
creating the look of a long fringe, and glue the two pieces
together.

4 Add dots of clear adhesive to the figure in unobtrusive
spots, such as the eyes and collar tips, to fix it to the inside of
the case. Allow to dry. Snap into position over your phone.

TIP/ You may need to adjust the size of the
girl in the template to fit your particular
phone case. You could do this by using
a photocopier to enlarge (or reduce) the
template, or by using a computer to scan
it and then enlarge (or reduce) the image
via your printer.

MOVABLE LETTER BUNTING

YOU WILL NEED:

Thin card (patterned or plain)
Nylon beading thread or fine string
Needle

TIP / Cut out a larger selection of letters to make a reusable garland. The letters can then be rearranged to create a sentiment suitable for any any occasion.

1 Print out (or hand draw) the letters and symbols of your choice, using a chunky font. Aim to make them 10–12cm (4–5in) high. You can choose initials, as shown, or spell out words.

2 Trace each letter onto patterned card and cut out, trimming just inside the traced line.

3 Use a needle to take your thread or string down through one side of the first letter, near the upper edge. Go across the back and then back up at the opposite side of the letter.

4 Slide the letter along to the end of the thread and repeat with a second. Add all of the remaining letters and symbols in the same way.

5 Pick a spot to hang the garland and then slide the letters around so they clearly spell out your chosen message.

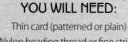

TIP / Vintage display signs, whether numbers or letters, can be hard to track down and are often costly. This is an easy and inexpensive way to get a similar look.

FAUX-VINTAGE NUMBER SIGN

YOU WILL NEED:

Corrugated card (e.g., cardboard grocery boxes)
Craft knife
PVA glue
Papier mâché powder
Fine sandpaper
Coloured tissue paper
Découpage medium
Small brush

TECHNIQUE: Découpage, Papier Mâché

1 Print or hand draw your chosen number (or letter) in a clear, blocky font. Trace onto a piece of corrugated card and cut out with a craft knife. Glue to a second piece of card. Cut out around the edges to make a double-layered card number.

2 Repeat, sticking the number to more layers of card and cutting out each in turn to build up depth. The number shown here is about 27cm (10½in) tall and made up of six layers. Adjust this to make your figure as tall as you like.

3 Mix up papier mâché powder following the packet instructions. Smooth it over the side edges of the card number and down into the corrugated card gaps. Set aside to dry. Rub gently with sandpaper to remove lumps or uneven patches.

4 Tear tissue paper into small pieces. Use découpage medium to stick them all over the cardboard number, overlapping edges and smoothing each piece flat. Add a second layer if you want darker, more intense colour.

DISPLAY BOBBINS

YOU WILL NEED:

Woodgrain-patterned tissue paper
Découpage medium
Empty bobbins or cotton reels
Patterned paper
Air-drying clay
Jewellery wire (26-gauge) or fuse wire
Scissors or pliers

TECHNIQUE: Découpage

TIP / Use the finished bobbins to hold place-cards on a dining table, or notes and photographs around the house.

1 Cut a circle of woodgrain tissue, 2–3cm (¾–1¼in) bigger all round than the top of your bobbin. Spread découpage medium over the bobbin top and stick the tissue into place.

2 Make slits about 1cm (⅜in) apart in the excess tissue around the edges. Spread découpage medium over the bobbin sides. Fold over each paper piece and press onto the glue. Use a craft knife to make similar slits across the centre hole. Fold and stick these inside. Repeat at the opposite end. (For a speedy alternative, omit steps 1 and 2 and use real vintage wooden bobbins instead.)

3 Snip a piece of patterned paper to fit around the centre of the bobbin (where the thread would usually be) and stick into place.

4 Roll a small piece of air-drying clay into a ball and push into the hole at one end of the bobbin (to fit quite snugly).

5 Cut 20cm (8in) of wire and wrap the centre three times around a pencil. Squeeze the wire ends together and slip into the hole in the centre of the bobbin. Push down into the clay ball to secure.

PAPER POMPOMS

YOU WILL NEED:
Card
Plain and patterned tissue papers
Sewing machine and thread

☆

TECHNIQUE: Sewing on Paper

1 Draw and cut out a circle of card 13cm (5in) diameter to use as a template. (You can adjust this measurement to make larger or smaller pompoms.)

2 Draw around your template onto pieces of plain and patterned tissue. Cut out 70–80 tissue paper circles in total.

TIP / Don't panic! You don't have to cut 70–80 circles one at a time. Layer multiple sheets of tissue together and cut up to ten circles at once.

3 Layer the circles on top of each other to make a neat bundle, lining up the edges as best you can.

4 Pull out a long length of thread (both bobbin and top threads) from your sewing machine – this will make it easier to hang your pompom later. Machine stitch along the centre of the bundle of circles to join them together.

5 One at a time, fold over the semicircular 'pages' on either side of the stitched line and gently scrunch the tissue paper between your fingers. This will fluff them up, adding body to the paper and turning a flat pile of paper into a dimensional sphere.

HIPSTER MERIT BADGES

YOU WILL NEED:

3cm (1¼in) diameter wooden discs
Circular badge cut-outs
PVA glue
Emery board
Brooch pins

1 Using the cut-outs provided, carefully cut out each of the badges that you want to use. Trim just outside the coloured edge, leaving a tiny white border all round.

2 Spread a thin layer of glue over the back of the badge, right out to the edges. Press down firmly onto the wooden disc. Leave to dry.

3 Gently sand around the outside with an emery board to smooth out the join between the paper and wood.

4 Squeeze a line of glue over the back of the brooch pin. Press into place on the back of the disc, about a third of the way down from the top. Allow to dry completely before wearing.

TIP / Use the guide on the cut-out sheet to identify each badge and then match it to the wearer's merits or interests.

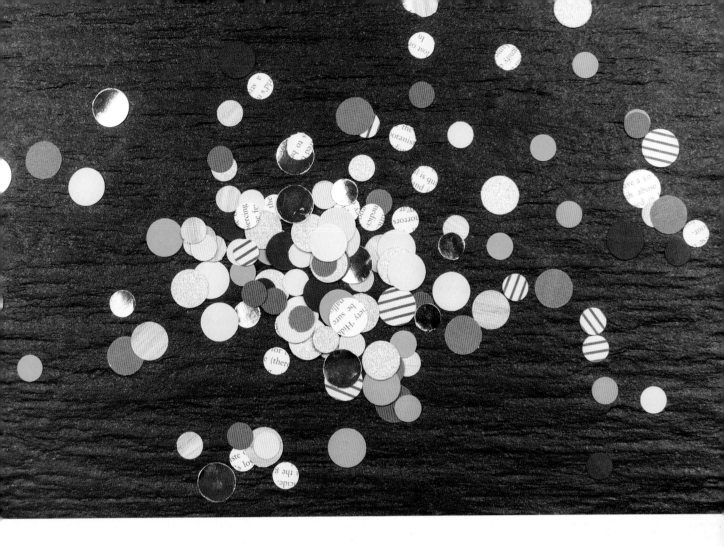

CUSTOM CONFETTI

YOU WILL NEED:

Plain and patterned papers
Circle punch(es)

☆

TIP / Papers that are only patterned or coated on one side can look a little odd in the finished pile of confetti. Try sticking a couple of sheets together, back to back, so they become double-sided. Allow the glue to dry before punching.

1 Gather together your selected papers. Try to pick mostly plains with a few small patterns, and maybe also a glitter or metallic sheet.

2 Punch out circles, keeping them very close together to get the maximum amount of confetti out of each sheet. Depending on paper thickness, you might be able to punch two or three layers at a time. You could use a single punch to create uniform pieces, or different ones for a mixture of sizes.

3 Tip the finished circles into a large bowl and mix so the various colours and sizes are thoroughly and randomly mixed together.

Alternative:

You could use some of your confetti to fill party balloons. Simply pour a small handful of pieces into a transparent balloon before inflating it.

TIP/ The templates are all simple, geometric shapes, so can be adjusted to fit larger or smaller tiles. Alternatively, use them as inspiration to build your own patterns.

WITH-OR-WITHOUT-A-BISCUIT COASTERS

YOU WILL NEED:

Ceramic tiles (square for just a mug, rectangular for mug and biscuit)
Plain and patterned tissue paper
Découpage medium
Small brush
Thick watercolour paper
PVA glue

TECHNIQUE: Découpage

1 Trace the templates for your chosen coaster onto tissue paper and cut out.

2 Spread a thin layer of découpage medium onto the surface of the tile. Take one of the tissue-paper pieces and place it gently down on top, using the template as a positioning guide. Smooth out the tissue with your fingers, so it's as flat as possible. Don't worry about smoothing fine wrinkles, as these are inevitable.

3 Fold the excess tissue down over the sides and onto the back of the coaster. Add some extra découpage medium to fix in place.

4 Add the remaining tissue-paper pieces in the same way and allow to dry. Brush two to three coats of découpage medium over the surface to seal and protect.

5 Cut a piece of thick watercolour paper, slightly smaller than the tile. Glue to the back, so your finished coaster won't scratch surfaces.

PAPER BALL WREATH

YOU WILL NEED:

Polystyrene or spun paper balls in a
selection of sizes
Coloured tissue paper
PVA glue or découpage medium
Large needle
Jewellery wire (14-gauge approx.)
Pliers (optional)
Ribbon

TIP / To create bolder or darker colours, add a
double layer of tissue (i.e., four pieces)
over each ball.

1 Take one of the paper balls and tear two pieces of tissue paper large enough to wrap around. Spread PVA or découpage medium over the back of the first piece and carefully smooth it onto the ball. Add the second in the opposite direction, so the smooth centre part goes over the scrunched ends of the first piece. Roll the ball between your palms to flatten out any lumps or wrinkles.

2 Repeat with the remaining balls, using a mixture of different tissue colours.

3 When the glue is dry, push a large needle all the way through the centre of each ball to make a threading hole.

4 Cut a 1m (1yd) length of strong wire and thread on the balls. You can mix up the colours randomly, or create blocks by grouping them together (as shown). When you're happy with the design and size of the wreath, bring the wire ends together, creating a circle. Twist the wire with pliers to secure, and snip off excess. Tie on a length of ribbon to cover the joins and create a hanging loop.

UPCYCLED SHOES

TECHNIQUE: Découpage

TIP / Weatherproof découpage medium will give your finished shoes a tough finish. Normal découpage medium works almost as well – just avoid wearing the shoes in wet weather.

1 Tear the tissue paper into small pieces. Spread découpage medium over a small area of shoe and place one of the pieces on top. Smooth it out with a brush or your fingers. Add a second piece in the same way, slightly overlapping the edges of the first. Keep going, filling up your chosen areas of the shoe (e.g., just the canvas parts on this pair).

2 When you reach the edges or an eyelet hole, take a tissue paper piece and, without adhesive, place it so it overlaps the edge. Run the tip of your scissors along the edge, tracing an indent onto the tissue. Take the tissue away, cut along the indented line and place back onto the shoe to check it fits neatly up against the edge or eyelet. Make any adjustments and then stick into place with découpage medium.

3 When you've covered the whole shoe, set aside to dry. Brush one to two extra coats of medium over the decorated areas of the finished pair to seal and protect them.

DIY DECO-TAPE

YOU WILL NEED:

Double-sided sticky tape in width(s) of your choice

Thin or lightweight patterned papers

TECHNIQUE: Découpage

1 Cut a length of double-sided tape and press down onto the back of your chosen paper.

2 Carefully cut along the edges of the tape with scissors or a craft knife and trim the ends to neaten. The tape is now ready to use. Try adding it to cards, wrapping around gifts and parcels, or using it to decorate the outside of a plain tea-light.

TIP / Small pieces of paper (e.g., security envelopes or pages of book text) are great for making shorter strips of tape. Use gift wrap or large tissue-paper sheets to make continuous lengths and rolls. Alternatively, join shorter pieces together by butting up the paper edges and pressing a continuous length of tape down on top (the joins will be visible when you use the tape).

ALPHABET BLOCKS

YOU WILL NEED:

Small block canvas
Matte gel medium or
découpage medium
Patterned paper napkins
Patterned paper
Thick card (e.g., mountboard)
Glue stick and PVA glue

TECHNIQUE: Papercutting

1 Brush a thin coat of gel medium over the top surface of the canvas.

2 Peel apart the napkin layers so you're just left with the upper, printed sheet. Press this down very gently onto the canvas, allowing an even amount to overhang on all sides. Pat it into place with your fingers or a soft brush, and flatten any wrinkles. Don't rub, as this is likely to tear the paper.

3 Brush gel medium over the side edges of the canvas. Snip away a V shape from each corner of the napkin and press down onto the sides of the canvas as before. Trim excess paper down to just 1–2cm (⅜–¾in), fold this over onto the back of the canvas and stick into place with more gel medium.

4 Print out or trace your chosen alphabet letter and transfer onto a piece of patterned paper. Glue to thick card and cut out with a craft knife. If you're using a decorative font, carefully cut out the inner, detailed parts of the letter, too. When the canvas is completely dry, glue the letter on top.

TIP / Pick either a bold, blocky font for your letters, or something decorative, such as a circus or folk-style typeface. (The one used here is called Venezuela.)

PAPER GIFT ROSETTE

YOU WILL NEED:

Patterned paper
PVA or glue stick
Double-sided tape

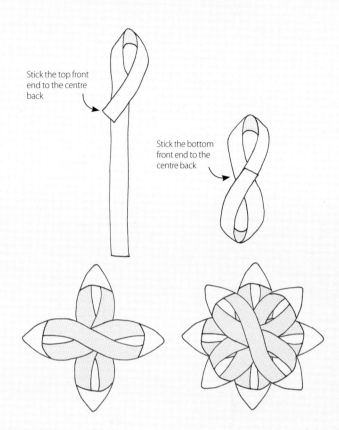

Stick the top front
end to the centre
back

Stick the bottom
front end to the
centre back

1 Cut nine strips of paper as follows: four 22 x 1.5cm (8½ x ⅝in); two 20 x 1.5cm (8 x ⅝in); two 18 x 1.5cm (7 x ⅝in); one 7 x 1.5cm (2¾ x ⅝in). Fold all but the smallest strip in half to find the centre.

2 Take a strip, fold the end round and stick to the back of the strip, over the creased centre line, as shown. Repeat with the other end.

3 Repeat with all folded strips. Curve the leftover 7cm (2¾in) strip around into a ring shape, overlap the ends and glue together.

4 To build the rosette, stick two of the largest folded strips together at right angles, as shown. Repeat with the two remaining large pieces. Layer on top of the first pair, so all eight points are evenly spaced.

5 Join the remaining pairs of strips together in the same way, sticking the smaller ones on top of the medium-sized set. Glue to the base section and add the small paper ring in the centre. Use double-sided tape to fix the rosette to a gift.

TIP / When choosing your paper, bear in mind that both sides will be visible on the finished rosette.

PARTY HATS

YOU WILL NEED:

Compass
Thin card
Patterned paper
Glue stick
Double-sided tape
Shirring elastic
Needle
Decorations (optional, see
Alternatives)

☆

1 Set your compass to 14cm (5½in) and draw a semicircle on thin card. Cut out and glue a piece of patterned paper on top. Trim away excess paper from the edges, so the card shape is neatly covered.

2 Roll the semicircle into a cone, overlapping the edges by about 5cm (¾in) at the bottom. Trace a line along the overlapped edge and then allow the cone to unfurl.

3 Cover the section inside the traced line with double-sided tape. Re-roll the cone, pressing the overlapped edge firmly down onto the tape.

4 Cut a length of elastic long enough to hold the hat on your head. Knot one end and use a needle to pierce a hole and thread it through one side of the hat, close to the bottom edge. Thread it back through on the opposite side, and then knot the other end.

5 Add a decoration of your choice to finish off, or leave plain.

Alternatives:

Decorate a hat by spreading a line of PVA glue around the bottom and then sprinkling with chunky glitter.

Glue a pompom to the top – perhaps made from paper raffia.

Stick a paper flower on the front.

TEAR-OUT MATCHBOOKS

YOU WILL NEED:

Thin card (plain or patterned)
Plain paper
Sewing machine or needle and craft foam
Embellishments or decorations (optional)

TECHNIQUE: Folding + Scoring, Sewing on Paper

1 Copy the cover template onto thin card and cut out. Score, then fold along the dotted lines. Using the pages template as a guide, print the details of your invitation onto plain paper and cut out.

2 To make the perforations, feed the paper pages through an unthreaded sewing machine, 'stitching' a line of holes 2cm (¾in) above the bottom edge of each one. (If you don't have a sewing machine, make the holes by hand using a sharp needle and a piece of foam under the paper.)

3 Gather the pages together in a neat bundle and place inside the cover, with the perforated lines just above the folded-over bottom flap (marked C on the template), so they can neatly be torn out when required. Staple through all layers.

4 Fold the front part of the cover over (marked A on template) and tuck the bottom edge behind the stapled flap to hold it closed. Add any (optional) extra decoration to the front cover to finish off.

TIP / The matchbooks shown are used as invitations, but you could fill the cover with plain pages instead, to make a matchbook notepad.

Anna & Peter
24·08·14

TIP/ Trace or copy the cut-out sheet before folding your box, and then use the copy as a template to create more boxes, with different types of patterned paper or card.

EASY-FOLD BOX

YOU WILL NEED:
Double-sided tape or glue stick

TECHNIQUE: Folding + Scoring

1 Cut around the outer edges of the box on the cut-out sheet provided.

2 Score, then fold, along the inner edges, as shown on the diagram.

3 Add double-sided tape or glue to the right side of each of the tabs. Stick each tab behind the corresponding box edge, as shown. Press the joins firmly together, so they're well stuck.

4 Fold the lid over the base to open and close the finished box. You can either use it to wrap a special gift, or to store tiny items (e.g. jewellery, accessories, paper clips, rubber bands).

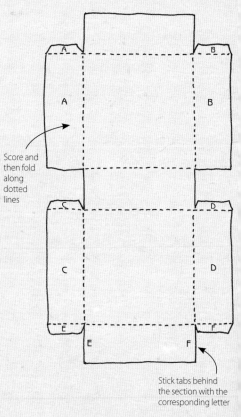

Score and then fold along dotted lines

Stick tabs behind the section with the corresponding letter

INSIDE OUT ENVELOPES

YOU WILL NEED:

Large security envelopes
(A5 or A4 size)
Glue stick

TECHNIQUE: Folding + Scoring

1 Cut along the side edges of a large security envelope to reveal the pattern inside. Copy the envelope template onto the plain white side of the envelope. Cut out and then score and fold along the dotted lines.

2 With the white side face up, fold the two sections marked C over onto section A. Spread glue over the patterned side of both C pieces. Fold section B over onto section A, so the two C pieces are sandwiched between. Press down firmly along the sticky edges.

3 Snip an envelope wrap from the cut-out sheet, cutting just outside the dotted lines. Glue to the front of the envelope, allowing about a quarter to overhang one edge. Fold this over and glue to the back of the envelope. Write the recipient's address on the front of the wrap and your return details on the smaller back section.

4 To seal the envelope, either apply glue directly to the flap (D) when you're ready to post it, or look out for special envelope glue, which allows you to 'lick and stick', just like store-bought envelopes.

TIP/ Use the same technique to fold envelopes from gift wrap. Make with the white side facing out and the pattern hidden inside as a pretty surprise for the recipient.

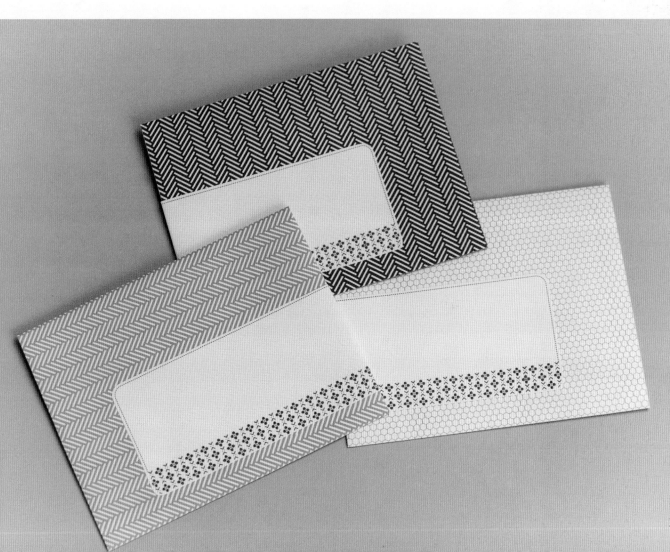

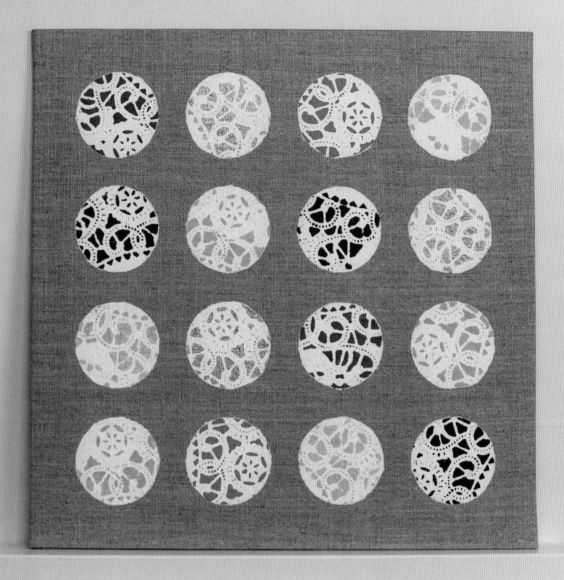

DOUBLE-STENCILLED DOTS

YOU WILL NEED:

Graph paper
Compasses
Repositionable adhesive
Canvas panel
Acrylic paint (white and selection of colours)
Paintbrush with firm bristles
Paper doilies
Cotton buds (cotton swabs) (optional)

1 Draw a grid of 16 large circles using a compass and graph paper to help you space them evenly apart. Cut each one out. Discard the circles, ready to use the negative space around them as a stencil.

2 Spray the back of the stencil with repositionable adhesive and press down onto the canvas background. Apply white paint to the canvas through the stencil. Use a brush with firm bristles and work with a pouncing or stabbing motion, rather than brushing on the paint.

3 When the paint is dry, cut 16 pieces of paper doily large enough to fit over the circular gaps in the stencil. Spray the backs with repositionable adhesive and place one over each gap.

4 Apply paint in different colours, pouncing it on over the doily, as before. Carefully lift off each piece of doily as soon as you've painted over it. Allow to dry. Peel away the dots stencil. Use a damp cotton bud (swab) to rub away any small pieces of paper that have clung to the painted edges of the spots.

TIP / Adjust the grid of dots, adding more or less, depending on the size of your canvas panel.

ARM CANDY BANGLES

YOU WILL NEED:

Wooden bangle(s)
Tissue paper
Découpage medium
Small brush

TECHNIQUE: Découpage

1 Tear the tissue paper into strips, long enough to wrap around the inside and outside faces of your bangle.

2 Spread découpage medium over a small section of the bangle (inside and out) and press a piece of tissue down on top. Gently smooth the surface with your fingers or a brush. Fold the ends over to the inside.

3 Repeat with a second piece of tissue, overlapping the edges with the first strip. Keep going until the whole bangle is covered. Set aside to dry.

4 Brush on one to two extra coats of medium to seal and protect your finished bracelet.

Alternatives:

Use vintage sewing-pattern tissue for a minimal but striking effect.

Decorate a narrow bangle with strips of paper washi tape, instead of tissue.

If you have a faceted bangle, cut panels of paper (e.g., old book text) to fit on each of the facets.

SEQUINS-IN-A-ROW CARD

YOU WILL NEED:

Plain card blank, 10 x 15cm (4 x 6in)
Sewing machine
Sewing thread to match card background
Sequins
Scrap of plain card
Alphabet stickers or letters cut from an old book (optional)
Washi tape

TECHNIQUE: Sewing on Paper

1 Open out the card blank flat. Place the centre fold under the foot of your sewing machine, make a few stitches, stop with the needle in the down position and then lift up the foot. Slide a sequin underneath, so it sits snugly against the needle. Lower the foot and make a few more stitches, this time going over the sequin. Repeat, adding more sequins one at a time until you reach the opposite edge of the card. Sew as many or as few lines as you like.

2 When you reach the last line, cut a narrow strip of card. Print, write or use stickers to add your message to the bottom half. Place the strip under the foot, as for the sequins, and sew along the top edge. Finish the rest of the line with sequins and stitches, as before.

3 Stick a length of washi tape over the back of each line of stitching, catching in the loose thread ends to secure and neaten the inside of the card.

Alternative:

For a different look, sew a vertical row of plain and shaped sequins instead. Use a simple heart shape cut from thin card in place of the sentiment strip.

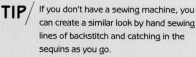

TIP / If you don't have a sewing machine, you can create a similar look by hand sewing lines of backstitch and catching in the sequins as you go.

COCKTAIL PARTY UMBRELLAS

YOU WILL NEED:

Plain or patterned paper
Compass or something circular to
draw around
Long cocktail sticks or satay skewers
Non-toxic marker pen
PVA glue

☆

TECHNIQUE: Folding + Scoring

1 Draw and cut out a 10cm (4in) diameter circle of paper. Fold it in half, then into quarters and finally into eighths.

2 Open the circle out – there will be 16 small sections, marked by fold lines. Cut out two of them and discard. Overlap the pieces on either side of the gap and glue them together to form an umbrella shape. Go around the paper circle and re-crease each fold line so they're all mountain folds.

3 Use a marker pen to draw stripes around the top part of a cocktail stick or satay skewer.

TIP / If satay skewers are too long, cut them down with a pair of sharp scissors. Glue the cut end inside the umbrella, so it's safely hidden from view.

4 Add a blob of glue to the apex of the umbrella, on the inside. Gently press the end of your decorated stick into the glue. Stand the umbrella upright (try pushing the end into a block of oasis or lump of plasticine) until the glue is completely dry.

CAMERA STORAGE BOX

YOU WILL NEED:

Small rectangular box with deep lid
Black and silver paint
Thick card (e.g., recycled from board-backed envelope)
Ribbed card and thin white card
Patterned papers and woodgrain-patterned paper
PVA glue
Marker pens

TECHNIQUE: Collage

1 Paint the box and lid black and allow to dry. Cut a strip of thick card slightly smaller than the top edge of the box and another about 5mm (¼in) smaller all round than the first. Glue together and paint black. Stick to the top edge of the box to add dimension.

2 Cut three strips of ribbed card 5mm–1cm (¼–⅜in) wide. Roll each one up, ridges on the outside, and glue the ends in place. Paint black, then brush silver paint on top. Glue to the top edge to make buttons and dials.

3 Wrap a strip of woodgrain paper around the the front and sides of the lid. Cut a narrower strip of white card and draw vertical lines along the edges. Add patterned paper on top. Stick over the woodgrain.

4 Roll up a 1cm (⅜in) wide strip of corrugated card for the lens, adding an extra strip of woodgrain paper around the outside. Cut a circle of white card to fit on top. Following the template, draw on the details. Glue the card to the lens and the lens to the lid. Cut a rectangle of light paper for the viewfinder and outline with a fine pen. Stick in the upper right-hand corner.

TIP / Use the finished box to store camera accessories (cables, SD memory cards, spare batteries and so on), or a collection of favourite photos.

STITCHED LOVE
PHOTOGRAPH

YOU WILL NEED:

Photograph
Tracing paper
Sheet of craft foam or mouse mat
Needle
Embroidery thread in two colours

TECHNIQUE: Sewing on Paper

1 Transfer the stitching template onto a sheet of tracing paper and place over your photograph. Make any necessary adjustments to the size or proportions of the heart by moving the outer points (marked with black dots) so the subject(s) of the photograph fit neatly inside. Keep the tracing paper on top of the photo and slip a sheet of craft foam underneath. Use a needle to pierce a hole through each of the corner points.

2 Sew from each point to the next, using a single, long stitch (worked like a very large form of backstitch). Change to a different thread colour and sew around the heart again, this time stitching over alternate points, e.g., instead of going from point 1 to 2, 2 to 3, 3 to 4, and so on, go from 1 to 3, 2 to 4, 3 to 5, and so on. Knot or tape the threads neatly at the back to secure.

3 Sew a selection of random cross stitches around the outer edges of the heart, either freehand, or by marking them on the tracing paper and piercing holes through the photo, as before.

TIP / Don't think the heart design is only suitable for wedding photos. It works just as well on shots of pets, friends, family members or even favourite places and landscapes.

THE OWL AND THE PUSSYCAT

TIP/ To display, you can either stand the finished board on a shelf, or glue a simple picture hook to the back and hang it on the wall.

YOU WILL NEED:

Dark grey or navy blue mountboard
35 x 16cm (13¾ x 6¼in)
Patterned papers (various, including glitter and shades of sea blue and pea green)
PVA glue
Two small matchboxes
Paper fasteners (brads)
Dowel stick or bamboo skewer
Aluminium foil
Paper clay
Acrylic paint and brush
Fine black marker pen

TECHNIQUE: Collage

1 Glue a 16 x 7.5cm (6¼ x 3in) rectangle of blue paper to the bottom of the mountboard and a 6cm (2⅜in) circle of glitter paper near the top.

2 Use the templates to cut boat pieces from pea green paper. Curve the strip around, sticking the slits to the back edges of one boat shape. Glue the boat to the background, hiding the slits.

3 Stick two matchboxes together and wrap paper around the outside. Remove the drawers. Glue the boxes to the centre of the boat, lining up bottom edges. Push paper fasteners through each side to secure to the background. Replace the drawers. Stick the second boat on top, gluing the slits of the joining strip to the outside back edges. Cut 13cm (5in) of dowel and glue to the background. Add an 11 x 7cm (4¼ x 2¾in) triangle for a sail and a tiny paper flag at the top.

4 Scrunch foil into two cylindrical body shapes. Cover each with a thin layer of paper clay. Mould tiny pieces of clay into ears and a tail, pressing into place on the models. When dry, paint the figures. Add faces with a marker pen. Glue into place on top of the matchboxes.

RECORD PLAYER INVITATION

YOU WILL NEED:

Large matchbox
Patterned papers
Glue stick
Thin card (black and white and silver)
Thick card
Fine black marker pen

TECHNIQUE: Collage

TIP / As a speedy alternative if you're making lots of invitations, construct the first one following the instructions, then scan or photocopy the deck section to make the rest.

1 Cut a strip of woodgrain paper the same width as the matchbox and long enough to wrap around it with ends overlapped. Glue to the outside of the box. Cut another piece to cover the ends and inside of the drawer and stick into position.

2 Use the template to cut out the pieces of the deck, resizing it to fit your matchbox, if needed. Glue the base on top of the matchbox, with the speaker panel at one end and turntable opposite (see diagram). Add the record on top of the turntable and the arm to the right. Draw on the speaker with a marker pen and add the slider and buttons to the panel.

3 Stick the final two buttons to the front edge of the box. Write or print out a name (i.e., the recipient's name or greeting), and glue to the opposite end as the brand name.

4 Make extra records to go inside the drawer. Cut out circles of white card the same size, printing or writing the details of your invitation on them. Glue one to the back of each circle.

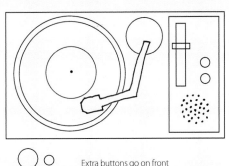

Extra buttons go on front edge of matchbox

DISC STORAGE ALBUM

YOU WILL NEED:

Mountboard or thick card
Patterned paper
Glue stick
Number or alphabet stickers (optional)
Clear, flexible CD sleeves
Hole punch
Two binder rings

TIP / Use the album to store films burned onto DVD, or CDs filled with photographs. If you back up photos once a month, the album is a perfect fit for a year's worth of CDs.

1 Cut a 15 x 18cm (6 x 7in) piece of thick card or mountboard, and two the same size from patterned paper. Glue a sheet of patterned paper to each side of the card. This is the front cover. Make the back cover in the same way.

2 Add optional decorations to the front cover, gluing on contrasting card and maybe giving your album a title, year or a number if you're planning to make multiple volumes.

3 For each 'page' cut a 10 x 13cm (4 x 5in) piece of patterned paper and fold in half. Apply a strip of glue along one edge, on the back of the card, and place the bottom of a clear CD sleeve down on top. Add glue to the rest of the card back, fold over and press down firmly. Make 11 more sleeves in the same way.

4 Punch holes in the card part of each sleeve, and corresponding ones in the front and back covers. Thread two large binder rings through all of the holes to join the album together.

PAPERED BOOKENDS

YOU WILL NEED:

Small china animal ornament
Block of wood or a small box
Dry rice or gravel (optional)
Sticky tape (optional)
Strong multi-purpose adhesive
White (or a pale/neutral) spray paint
Patterned tissue paper
Découpage medium
Small paintbrush

TECHNIQUE: Découpage

TIP You can either make a single bookend or a pair. Don't worry if you can't find two identical ornaments – the patterned paper will help to coordinate a mismatched pair.

1 Glue the animal to a block of wood or small box. If using a box, fill with dry rice or gravel to weigh it down and then seal shut with sticky tape.

2 Cover the whole thing with two to three coats of white spray paint and set aside to dry.

3 Tear the patterned tissue into pieces of various sizes – from very small to fit around the more detailed parts of the ornament, to larger pieces for the flat base. Use découpage medium to stick the pieces onto the painted bookend. Press the paper down firmly, smoothing over the edges and making sure it's as flat as possible. Use a small brush to help push the paper neatly into nooks and crannies. Overlap the edges of the pieces as you apply them and keep going until the whole thing is covered.

4 When the découpage medium is dry, brush on one to two additional coats to seal and protect.

CUT-OUT TANGRAMS

YOU WILL NEED:

Thin card or a folded card blank
Craft knife
Patterned paper
Glue stick

TECHNIQUE: Papercutting

1 Trace your chosen tangram template onto thin card to make a piece of wall art, or a folded card blank to make a greetings card. Use a craft knife to carefully cut away the shaded areas, leaving a series of gaps or apertures.

2 To add pattern behind each cut-out section, snip a piece of patterned paper slightly larger all round than the aperture. On the back of the card, spread glue around the gap's edges. Press the paper face down over the glue so the pattern shows on the front. Fill each of the apertures using a mixture of patterns and colours to build up a design you like.

3 Copy the non-shaded sections of the template onto separate pieces of pattered paper and cut each one out. Stick the pieces over their respective areas on the background.

4 To finish off, print or write a simple sentiment onto a scrap of paper, cut out and stick on the card front.

TIP / A tangram is a Chinese puzzle made up of seven geometric shapes that can be rearranged to form different images, such as the bird and chevron shown. Why not use the shapes to create your own pictures or designs.

HOLA

ENVELOPE ORGANIZER

TECHNIQUE: Folding + Scoring

1 Transfer the envelope template onto the back of patterned paper. Score along the lines, as marked, and cut out around the outline. Cut a contrasting piece of paper 23.8 x 17cm (9⅜ x 6¾in) and glue over centre section (A). Make two more envelopes in the same way.

2 Fold the B, C and D flaps of each envelope in towards the centre, but don't stick down yet. Space the envelopes evenly on the board. Spread glue over the back of section A on each envelope and press into position on the board. Open out the flaps and push a paper fastener through each side of section A.

3 Fold flap D up over section A. Spread glue onto the back of flaps B and C (shaded areas on template) and press down firmly over flap D.

4 Copy the label templates onto thin card and cut out. Write a name or title on the rectangular one and glue behind the holder. Fix each label to the envelope centre using tiny paper-fasteners.

TIP / Use the finished envelopes to hold letters, notes, bills, invitations and so on. Cut a double-width board and fold three extra envelopes to add even more storage space.

DIY GIFT WRAP

YOU WILL NEED:

Plain gift wrap or brown parcel paper
Stamp and ink
Fine marker pen (optional)
Paint pen (optional)

TECHNIQUE: Sewing on Paper

1 You can either decorate a roll to use when required, or a smaller piece big enough to wrap a specific present. Spread the paper out flat. To stamp a regular, repeated pattern, measure out and draw a grid of faint pencil lines (to be erased later). Alternatively, judge the pattern by eye, or create a more random design.

2 Ink up your stamp and begin making impressions, using the grid as a positioning guide. To avoid smudging, work from left to right if you're right-handed, and vice versa if left-handed.

3 Make a few extra impressions on some scrap paper, to experiment with adding extra details. Try outlining the stamped shape with a fine marker, doodling on top of it with a paint pen, or using it as the basis for a larger motif (the flower pattern shown was built up from a circular stamp). Once happy with your design, add it to each of the stamped impressions on the paper.

TIP / For a design that's quick and simple, but still stylish, stamp random dots with the eraser end of a pencil (as shown in the black and white print).

TIP/ You can hang the finished ball as a decoration or use it as an alternative to a pomander-style bridesmaid's bouquet at a wedding (especially good for bridesmaids with hay-fever!).

PAPER SEQUIN BALL

YOU WILL NEED:

Hole punch or small circle punch
Patterned papers in coordinating colours
Craft foam or old mouse mat
Embossing stylus or medium-sized crochet hook
Polystyrene ball
Pins for sequins
String/twine or narrow ribbon
PVA glue

1 Punch small circles of patterned paper (about 400 for a 10cm/4in ball).

2 Place one of the circles, face up, on a sheet of craft foam. Run an embossing stylus or the pointed end of a crochet hook around the edge of the circle a few times, pressing down firmly. Gradually move it in towards the centre, still working in a circle. The flat paper should start curving into a sequin-like, cup shape. Set it aside, and repeat with the rest of the circles to make a large pile of paper sequins.

3 Place a sequin on the polystyrene ball and push a pin through the centre to hold in place. Add a second sequin next to the first, keeping them as close together as possible. Keep going, adding more sequins in the same way.

4 When you've almost covered the ball, take a length of string or narrow ribbon and glue the ends to the bare polystyrene. Pin more sequins into place over the glued ends, until the entire ball is covered.

PAPERVILLE

YOU WILL NEED:
Thin white card
PVA glue
Washi or masking tape
Black paper
Coloured and patterned papers

☺

TECHNIQUE: Scoring + Folding

TIP / To make the paned, sash-style windows, use four tiny pieces of black paper, glued beside each other with strips of white space between.

1 Decide on the type of building you want to create, and then work out how many blocks and which kind of blocks you will need to construct it. Use the diagram here as a guide or invent your own alternatives.

2 Copy the cube and/or rooftop templates onto thin, white card. Cut out, then score and fold along the lines, as marked. Spread glue over the tabs and fold into shape. Stick each tab behind the corresponding straight edge. Add strips of washi tape to hold the edges in place as the glue dries.

3 Glue the pieces together to form the building. Alternatively, stack them without adhesive, so they can be re-built as and when you like.

4 To make windows and doors, cut out pieces of black paper. Arrange in an even pattern (or randomly) and glue to the front of the building.

5 Cut coloured and patterned paper to decorate the roofs. Fold rectangles in half for the gabled rooftop pieces and stick on simple squares for flat roofs.

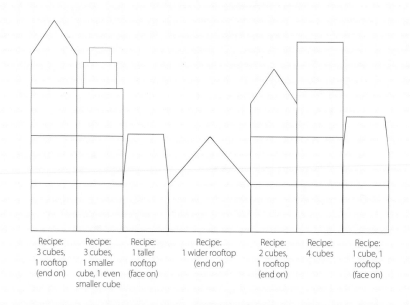

Recipe:
3 cubes,
1 rooftop
(end on)

Recipe:
3 cubes,
1 smaller
cube, 1 even
smaller cube

Recipe:
1 taller
rooftop
(face on)

Recipe:
1 wider rooftop
(end on)

Recipe:
2 cubes,
1 rooftop
(end on)

Recipe:
4 cubes

Recipe:
1 cube, 1
rooftop
(face on)

CHALKBOARD GIFT TAGS

YOU WILL NEED:

Thick card
Blackboard paint
Small brush
Black marker pen
Patterned paper
Hole punch
Eyelets and an eyelet-setting tool (optional)
Ribbon or string

TIP Add a note to the back of the tag to let the recipient know it is reusable. You could also pass on your chalk, so they can wipe the tag and re-address it.

1 Copy your chosen tag template onto thick card and cut it out using a sharp craft knife.

2 Add two to three coats of blackboard paint to one side of the tag, allowing each one to dry before brushing on the next. Use a black marker pen to colour the edges of the tag to match (it's quicker and less messy than trying to paint them).

3 Glue a decorative strip or piece of patterned paper to the front of the tag, using the template as a guide. Stick a plain piece of paper to the back for a neat finish.

4 Punch a hole at the top of the tag and add an (optional) eyelet. You can do this with a Crop-A-Dile, or traditional eyelet setting tool (see Materials & Equipment). Thread a length of ribbon or string through the hole to tie the tag to your parcel. Use chalk to write the recipient's name or a simple message on the front of the tag.

TIP / To create a different look, cut the spots from plain tissue, either in a mix of colours or a single shade.

PAPIER MÂCHÉ DOTS BOWL

YOU WILL NEED:

Small flexible plastic bowl (e.g., from a pre-packaged salad)
White tissue paper
Wallpaper paste
Small brush
Patterned tissue
Découpage medium

TECHNIQUE: Papier Mâché

1 Wash the bowl, dry thoroughly and turn it upside down. The outside will act as the mould for your paper bowl.

2 Tear the tissue paper into small pieces. Spread a thin layer of wallpaper paste over the back of the first one and smooth down onto the outside of the bowl. Add a second piece in the same way, slightly overlapping the first. Keep going to cover the outside of the bowl in a layer of paper strips. Leave to dry.

3 Add five or six more layers in the same way, to create a strong, opaque structure. When completely dry, slip the plastic bowl out and discard.

4 Cut pieces of plain or patterned tissue into small circles of various sizes, cutting them freehand for a random look. Stick the spots to the bowl, using a thin layer of découpage medium.

5 When the medium is dry, brush one to two additional coats over the whole bowl, to seal and protect it.

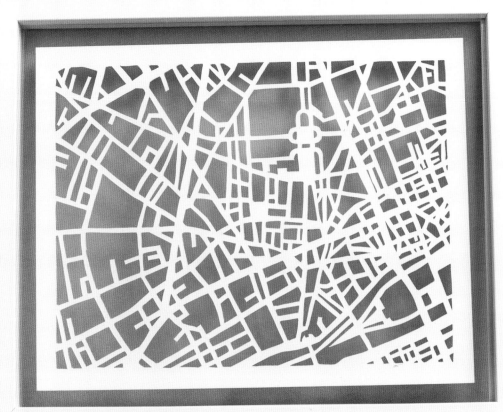

PAPERCUT MAP

1 Choose the section or page of the map you want to work with, perhaps the area where you live, or somewhere special you love visiting. Print, copy or trace it onto the reverse of a sheet of white card, leaving a narrow border around the outside.

2 Place on a cutting mat and use a craft knife to cut along the edges of the streets marked on the map. Take your time and work methodically across the map. As you cut, discard the non-street sections, i.e., areas filled with buildings, green spaces or water. When you've finished, turn the map over to reveal the white front side. Use the knife to neaten up rough areas (it's often easier to spot these from the front).

3 To display the finished papercut, mount in a floating frame, as shown, or slip a piece of card in a contrasting colour behind it and place in a standard picture frame.

YOU WILL NEED:

Street map (e.g., an A to Z)

Plain white card

Cutting mat

Craft knife

Floating frame (optional)

TECHNIQUE: Papercutting

TIP Bear in mind the map will be reversed when you cut it out. To avoid this, flip the image before transferring it onto the back of the paper.

PERPETUAL CALENDAR

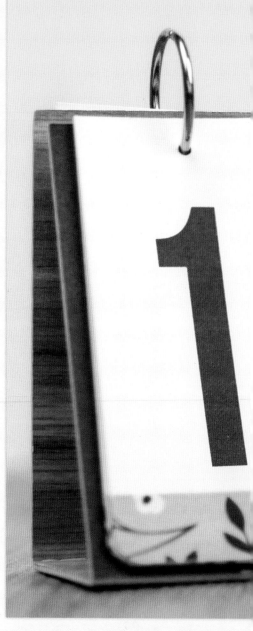

TECHNIQUE: Folding + Scoring

1 Cut a 23 x 25cm (9 x 10in) piece of mountboard and stick patterned paper to the back. Score two lines, as in the diagram, and punch four holes along each edge. Fold the punched edges in towards each other, forming the triangular shape of the calendar.

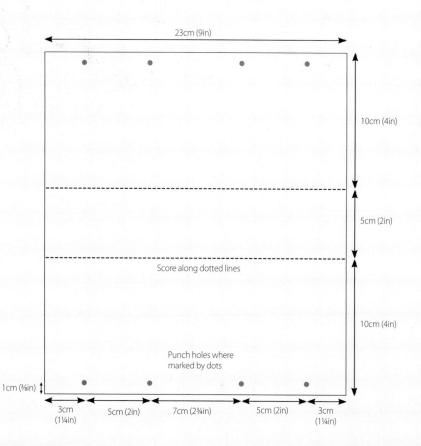

23cm (9in)

10cm (4in)

5cm (2in)

Score along dotted lines

10cm (4in)

Punch holes where marked by dots

1cm (⅜in)

3cm (1¼in)   5cm (2in)   7cm (2¾in)   5cm (2in)   3cm (1¼in)

TIP To make the finished calendar extra-durable, stick ring reinforcers over the punched holes in each card.

2 Cut 26 pieces of thin card, each 5 x 10cm (2 x 4in). Use the chart to add a number to each one; you can do this with number stickers, stamps or print them onto the card before cutting out. Glue a 1.5cm (⅝in) strip of patterned paper along the bottom edge of each card.

3 Punch a hole in the centre of each card, about 1cm (⅜in) below the top. If desired, use a corner-rounder to round the corners at the bottom. Thread a binder ring through each pair of holes in the base. The hinge must sit between the two holes, with the opening ends at the top.

4 Add number cards to each ring, as follows: left-hand ring 0–3; next 0–9; next 0–1; right-hand ring 0–9. Close the binder rings and flip the cards to display the date – the pair on the left showing the day and the pair on the right showing the month.

Note: For those used to the American system, add number cards to each ring in the following order: left-hand ring, 0–1; next, 0–9; next, 0–3, right-hand ring, 0–9.

Number Chart

No.0	No.1	No.2	No.3	No.4	No.5	No.6	No.7	No.8	No.9
Cut 4	Cut 4	Cut 3	Cut 3	Cut 2	Cut 2	Cut 2	Cut 2	Cut 2	Cut 2

SUCCULENT PLANTERS

YOU WILL NEED:

Thin white card A4
Patterned paper (e.g., gift wrap)
Double-sided tape
Small plastic bag (optional)

TECHNIQUE: Folding + Scoring

TIP / These indoor-only containers are perfect for succulents or other plants similar to cacti that don't require much watering. If you don't grow houseplants, use the container to collect and store small accessories on a desk or dressing table instead.

1 Glue patterned paper onto a sheet of thin white card. When the glue is dry, copy the template onto the card and cut around the outside.

2 Score and then fold along the dotted lines. Add a strip of double-sided tape to each of the tabs.

3 Peel away the tape backing, one piece at a time, as you fold the planter into shape. Use the template as a guide to help you stick each tab behind the corresponding straight edge, matching letter to letter. Press the joins firmly together, so they're well adhered.

4 Place a small plastic bag inside the finished container to stop it getting damp. Leave your succulent in its original plant pot and place carefully inside the container.

BOOK + MAGAZINE MARKERS

YOU WILL NEED:

Patterned paper

TIP/ For the patterned paper try gift wrap, re-purposed book or magazine pages, security envelopes and leaflets.

1 Cut a 10cm (4in) square of paper and fold it in half diagonally. With the long, straight edge at the bottom, fold the right-hand point of the triangle up to meet the centre point (see diagram). Press firmly along the folded edge to create a sharp crease. Repeat with the left-hand point of the triangle.

2 Undo the last two folds, so you're back to a triangle again. Working with the upper layer of paper only, fold the top point of the triangle down to meet the centre of the bottom edge. Press firmly along the fold.

3 Fold the right-hand point of the triangle up to the meet the centre point again. Now tuck it down behind the folded 'flap' you made before. Repeat with the left-hand point of the triangle. Finish by pressing firmly along the upper, folded edge of the pocket you've just created.

Alternative:

To turn the page markers into gifts or party favours, make a set in coordinating colours and slip into a clear plastic bag. Cut a square of paper the same width as the bag, fold in half and staple to the top edge. Decorate any way you like.

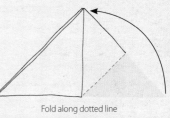

Fold along dotted line

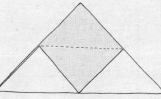

Fold along dotted line

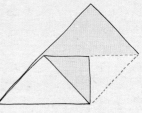

Fold along dotted line

MAGNETIC MEMO CLIPS

YOU WILL NEED:

Clothes pegs (clothespins)
Patterned paper
PVA glue
Thick card (e.g., mountboard)
Circular decals (from cut-out sheet)
Emery board
PVA glue
Small magnets

TIP / Use the finished pegs to fix notes, photos, cards invitations and children's art to your fridge or a magnetic board.

1 Measure the front of a clothes peg and cut a strip of paper to fit on top. Spread glue over the back of the paper, taking particular care around the edges. Press it firmly down onto the peg.

2 Draw and cut out a 2cm (¾in) diameter circle of thick card. Cut a circular decal (from the cut-out sheet), trimming just outside the coloured edge to leave a tiny white border all round. Glue the decal to the circle of card. Leave to dry, then gently sand around the edges with an emery board for a neat, smooth finish.

3 Stick the decorated circle to the front of the peg, about a quarter of the way up from the bottom.

4 Turn the peg over and glue a small magnet to the back. Make sure the glue is completely dry before using.

Alternative:

For a different look, glue a gem, button or paper flower to the front of the peg instead of using a circular decal.

TRANSPARENT FAVOUR ENVELOPES

YOU WILL NEED:

Transparent paper, such as vellum or glassine
Double-sided tape
Patterned papers
Sewing machine or needle and thread

TECHNIQUE: Sewing on Paper

1 Copy the template onto transparent paper. Cut around the outside edges and score along the marked dotted lines.

2 Fold sections A and B over section C and stick A and B together where they overlap, using double-sided tape. Fold section D upwards, onto the newly joined A and B, and stick into place with tape.

3 Fill the envelope with your chosen party favours and then fold over flap E at the top edge.

4 Layer together pieces of patterned paper (or you could use a photograph instead), and position near the top folded edge. Stitch by hand or machine along the top of the envelope, sewing the flap shut and fixing the decorative paper pieces in place at the same time.

TIP / These envelopes are perfect for holding small favours, such as sweets, seeds or jewellery. The template can easily be enlarged to hold larger quantities or bigger favours.

PAPER KITE

YOU WILL NEED:

40cm (16in) and 50cm (20in) dowel stick
Clear nylon beading thread or fishing line
Craft knife
Large sheet of paper
Glue stick or double-sided tape
White string
Patterned paper

1 Use nylon thread to tie the sticks together in a cross. With a craft knife, cut a horizontal notch in each stick's flat end. Cut 150cm (60in) of thread, tie a loop a little way from one end and place in the top notch. Pass the thread through each notch in turn, all round and back to the top, making a second loop at the bottom notch (see diagram). Knot the ends together and trim excess.

2 Lay the kite frame on the back of the paper, draw around it, adding a 3cm (1¼in) border all round and cut out. Fold all four sides over the string frame, cut away excess at corners and stick the folded edges in place.

3 Cut 50cm (20in) of white string for a tail and tie one end to the bottom loop of the kite. Make three paper bows (see Paper Bow Garland) and tape along the string.

4 Cut 60cm (24in) of nylon thread. Tie one end to the top loop of the kite. Where the two sticks cross, make another loop and tie the other end of the thread to the loop at the bottom edge. Tie a very long nylon thread to the loop in the kite centre to finish.

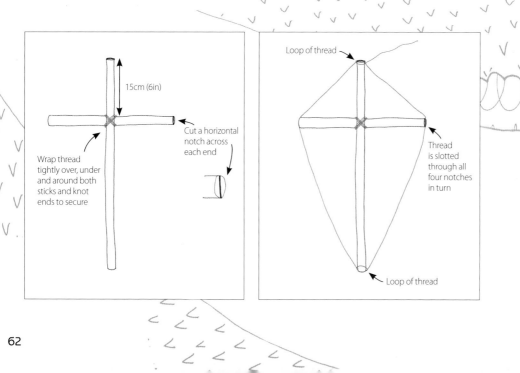

15cm (6in)

Cut a horizontal notch across each end

Wrap thread tightly over, under and around both sticks and knot ends to secure

Loop of thread

Thread is slotted through all four notches in turn

Loop of thread

FLYING BIRDS

YOU WILL NEED:

Faux bois or woodgrain-
patterned paper
Contrasting patterned paper
Glue stick
Needle and fine thread

TECHNIQUE: Folding + Scoring

1 Copy the bird template onto woodgrain paper and cut out twice. Score and fold along the edge of each bird wing, as marked. Copy the wing template onto patterned paper and cut out.

2 Apply glue to the back of one of the bird pieces, spreading it below the folded line only. Press the second bird on top, joining the bodies together, back to back.

3 Fold a length of thread in half and knot the ends together. Feed the folded end through the eye of a needle and then bring it up through the centre of the wing (as marked on template), so the knot sits snugly against the back of the paper.

4 Spread glue over the back of the patterned wing piece. Open out the wings at the top of the body and press the patterned piece down on top, so the edges are neatly aligned. Allow the glue to dry before hanging up the finished bird.

TIP / Adjust the template to make birds in a range of sizes. Use different thread lengths to hang them at varying heights.

FINGER PUPPETS IN COSY JUMPERS

YOU WILL NEED:

Finger puppet cut-outs
PVA glue

TIP / Check the cone fits your finger before gluing the edges together. Wrap it more tightly if you have tiny fingers, or make it looser for large hands.

1 Cut out each of the pieces from the cut-out sheet at the back of the book.

2 To make each cone-shaped sweater, spread a thin layer of glue over the non-patterned section of the cut-out semicircle. Curve the semicircle round, so the right-hand edge overlaps the non-patterned left edge. Press down onto the glue to secure. Try using a clothes peg (clothespin) to hold the pieces together as the glue dries.

3 Decide which sweater you want each animal to wear and glue the head to the top of its respective cone. Stick some of the heads on straight and tilt others at a slight angle for variety of expression. Allow the glue to dry before using the puppets.

MINI SUITCASE STORAGE

YOU WILL NEED:

Thick corrugated card
Glue gun
Tissue paper
Wallpaper paste or PVA glue
Acrylic paint (optional)
Metallic paint
Floral patterned paper
Medium-weight card
Woodgrain or metallic paper
Strong card (e.g., grungeboard)
Paper fasteners/brads

TECHNIQUE: Papier Mâché

1 Cut a 17 x 22cm (6¾ x 8¾in) rectangle of corrugated card and round the corners. Cut a strip 7 x 80cm (2¾ x 31½in). Squeeze hot glue around the rectangle's corrugated edges (not the flat surface) and press the strip onto the glue, wrapping it all round to form a box. Snip off excess, so the ends meet.

2 Repeat, with a 18 x 23cm (7 x 9in) rectangle and 3 x 85cm (1⅛ x 33½in) strip to make the lid. Cover both pieces with three layers of torn tissue papier mâché pieces. Use coloured paper for the final layer, or paint. Cut the floral paper 17.5 x 22.5cm (6⅞ x 8⅞in), round the corners and glue to the lid.

3 Use the template to cut and fold two handles in medium-weight card. Glue together, back to back, leaving shaded sections free. Cover with woodgrain or metallic paper. Cut two slits in the front of the case, feed the handle ends through, fold over and glue to the inside.

4 Cut two 3 x 4cm (1⅛ x 1½in) pieces of strong card for hinges. Cover with metallic paint. Use four paper fasteners to secure to the back of the case.

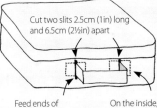

Cut two slits 2.5cm (1in) long and 6.5cm (2½in) apart

Feed ends of handle through the slits

On the inside, fold one strip end to the left and one to the right, and glue to secure

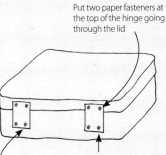

Put two paper fasteners at the top of the hinge going through the lid

Rectangles of strong card to make hinges

Put two paper fasteners at the bottom of the hinge going through the base

TIP You can use a pre-made box with a lid (e.g., shoebox) to make a similar case. Add a handle and hinges in the same way and finish off with smart cardboard corner protectors.

POLAROID CHARMS

YOU WILL NEED:

White mountboard, or similar
thick card

Craft knife

Computer and printer or
pre-printed mini photos

PVA glue

Metal bail

Plain necklace/chain or key ring

TECHNIQUE: Jewellery

1 Copy the polaroid template onto mountboard and carefully cut it out with a craft knife. Cut an extra 3 x 4cm (1¼ x 1½in) piece from the same board.

2 Choose a photo for your frame and print out so it measures 3cm (1¼in) square. Cut it out and then glue behind the aperture in the polaroid. Stick the plain piece of mountboard to the back, so the photograph is sandwiched in between.

3 Glue a metal bail to the back of the card, in the centre of the top edge.

4 Allow the glue to dry thoroughly and then thread the finished charm onto a necklace or key ring.

TIP / To make the charm a little tougher, especially if it's going to be used as a key ring, brush on a few coats of clear varnish.

SIMPLE EMBOSSED STATIONERY

YOU WILL NEED:

Plain sheets of writing paper
Scrap paper
Stamps
Ink
Embossing powder
Heat tool
Envelopes

TECHNIQUE: Stamping + Embossing

1 Place scrap paper over a sheet of plain writing paper, 2–3cm (¾–1¼in) up from the bottom edge. Ink up your chosen stamp and begin making impressions on the strip of writing paper visible below the scrap piece. Stamp in a variety of directions to build up a pattern, and don't be afraid to overlap the side edges as well.

2 When you've covered the whole strip, lift away the scrap paper and sprinkle embossing powder over the images. Shake off excess and heat to emboss.

3 Repeat, decorating as many sheets as you like, using a mixture of colours or stamps for variety. If the heat embossing makes the paper's edges curl, allow them to cool and then place under a stack of heavy books for a few hours.

4 To make coordinating envelopes, use a label stamp. Make impressions directly onto the envelope, or stamp on plain paper and cut the labels out individually. Decorate with an extra stamped impression, or stamp a pattern around the outside of the label instead.

TIP / For a subtle, textured effect, try using white embossing powder on white paper.

PAPER CLAY NAPKIN RINGS

YOU WILL NEED:

Plastic wrap
Paper clay, allow 100–120g (3½–4oz) per ring
Rolling pin
Scrap paper
Small vegetable or paring knife
Woodgrain stamp
Tiny alphabet stamps
Cardboard tube
Patterned paper
PVA glue

TECHNIQUE: Stamping + Embossing

1 Roll out 120g (4oz) of paper clay to about 5mm (¼in) thick on plastic wrap. Cut a 15 x 5.5cm (6 x 2⅛in) piece of paper as a template and place on top of the clay. Cut around the edges with a small knife. Discard the paper and set aside excess clay. Smooth the edges of the clay rectangle with a wet finger.

2 Tear a scrap of paper, roughly 1 x 2cm (⅜ x ¾in) and place in the centre of the clay. Press the woodgrain stamp down firmly on the clay, starting at one end of the rectangle. Lift off and repeat to make a second impression beside the first, adding more if necessary. Remove the scrap of paper, and in the gap add 'X O X O' or your chosen sentiment using tiny alphabet stamps.

3 Pick up the plastic wrap and clay and wrap it around a cardboard tube. Press the ends gently together. Leave to dry, according to the clay packaging instructions.

4 To finish, cut a strip of patterned paper and glue around the inside of the ring.

TIP/ If you can't find a woodgrain stamp, try pressing an actual piece of wood with a prominent grain down onto the clay instead.

PAPIER MÂCHÉ FRIDA

YOU WILL NEED:

Thick card
Craft knife
Papier mâché powder
Tissue paper white and red patterned
Paints in flesh-tone, white, pink and gold
Black and red marker pens
Paper flowers

TECHNIQUE: Papier Mâché

TIP / I chose to make a papier mâché tribute to Mexican artist, Frida Kahlo, but you can use the same technique to create a portrait of anyone – a friend, family member or favourite artist.

1 Copy the template outline onto thick card and cut out with a craft knife.

2 Mix up papier mâché powder following the instructions on the packaging. Smooth a layer, roughly 1cm (⅜in) thick over the front of the card. Snip a tiny triangle of card for a nose, fold in half and press gently down into the paste.

3 Allow the papier mâché to dry thoroughly. Add a layer of torn tissue papier mâché strips over the top, folding around onto the back of the shape, to create smooth, neat edges.

4 When the strips are dry, decorate the plaque. Brush on two coats of flesh-toned paint. Using the sketch as a guide, draw on hair, clothing and facial features in pencil. Fill in the eyes with white paint and use a tiny bit of pink for cheeks. Draw on pupils, eyebrows and hair with a black marker pen. Use a red marker for the lips.

5 Glue on a small piece of red patterned tissue to make a shirt. Paint a black shawl over the top. Use gold paint and the end of a cocktail stick to paint the chain necklace. Finally, glue paper flowers to the top of the head.

KOKESHI DOLLS

YOU WILL NEED:

Wooden head bead
Dolly-peg
PVA glue
Double-sided tape
Fine black marker pen
Patterned papers
Peach or pink marker pen
Nail polish
Paper flower decoration (optional)

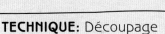

TECHNIQUE: Découpage

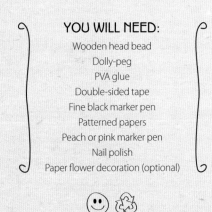

TIP/ Head beads are similar to normal wooden beads, but have a large hole drilled in one side. Search for them (or just plain wooden kokeshi figures) online.

1 Glue a wooden head bead to the top of a dolly-peg. When dry, draw on a face with a fine marker and add cheeks in pink pen. Draw the hairline in pencil.

2 Tear the paper for the hair into tiny pieces. (Old magazine pages are perfect for this.) Spread découpage medium inside the hairline. Press paper pieces on top, one at a time, overlapping the edges and smoothing them flat.

3 Cut a strip of paper long enough to wrap around the length of the peg. Overlap the ends at the back and glue together. Cut a rectangle of contrasting paper and snip a small piece off each short end so it's narrower at the top edge than at the bottom. Add double-sided tape along the inside of the top edge and wrap around the upper body, fixing it at the front.

4 Paint a line of nail polish around the base of the peg for shiny shoes (or use a black marker). Glue a paper flower to the head as an optional hair decoration.

BOX DISPLAY SHELVES

YOU WILL NEED:

Empty box
Large sheet of foam-core
Craft knife
PVA glue
Torn paper strips
Wallpaper paste
Small brush
Paint (spray, acrylic or emulsion)
Patterned paper (e.g., gift wrap or wallpaper)

TECHNIQUE: Papier Mâché

1 Place the box on the foam-core, draw around one side and cut out with a craft knife. Glue the foam-core to the box. Repeat on opposite side.

2 Repeat with the two remaining sides, this time drawing around the box, plus the two added pieces of foam-core. Draw around the back of the box, cut out one last piece of foam-core and glue in place.

3 Cover the outside of the box with several layers of papier mâché to strengthen and smooth over the joins. Allow to dry. Now apply two to three coats of paint.

4 To cover the inside, mark a rectangle the same size as the back of the box on the patterned paper. Score along the marked lines. Cut out, leaving a 1cm (⅜in) border all round. Fold along the scored lines and glue into the back of the box. Repeat to cover two of the box sides, this time folding over a border at the two shorter edges only. Finally, cut precise rectangles (no borders) to fit the remaining two sides and glue into position.

TIP / To hang your finished shelves, fix a plate-hanger to the back using strong adhesive or, if you want them to support heavier items, screw directly to the wall instead.

PATTERNED PICTURE MOUNTS

YOU WILL NEED:

Patterned paper
Picture mount
Spray adhesive or glue stick
Craft knife

TIP / There is a ready-to-frame version of the bear illustration on the cut-out sheet. Snip a simple bow shape from patterned paper and glue to the bear as an extra-fancy finishing touch.

1 Cut a piece of patterned paper, roughly 3cm (1¼in) larger all round than your picture mount. Smooth it out, face down, on a hard, flat surface.

2 Spread or spray glue all over the front of the picture mount and carefully place it on top of the paper. Turn the paper over and press down, smoothing it out firmly and evenly over the surface of the mount. Set aside to dry.

3 Cut away a triangle of paper across each of the outer corners, fold the edges over onto the back of the picture mount and stick down. Use a craft knife to cut an X across the inner aperture of the mount, from corner to corner. Snip out excess paper from the centre as shown, fold over the edges and glue to the back.

4 Use with a picture frame in the usual way, coordinating the patterned paper with simple illustrations or typographic images.

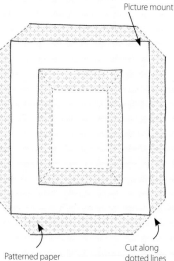

Picture mount

Patterned paper

Cut along dotted lines

WILD THINGS MASK

YOU WILL NEED:

Thin card
Patterned papers
Glue stick
Glitter paper
Large needle
Shirring or very thin elastic

1 Copy the mask template onto thin card and cut out. Fold it in half to create a prominent crease down the centre.

2 Trace around the card shape onto patterned paper and cut out again. Glue the paper piece on top of the card.

3 Copy the upper section of the template onto a contrasting piece of patterned paper and the edging strip onto glitter paper. Cut both out. Glue the edging strip to the back of the patterned paper, so it's just visible from the front. Stick the whole upper section on top of the paper-covered mask.

4 Cut a piece of shirring elastic long enough to wrap around the sides of your head. Use a large needle to thread one end through each side of the mask at eye level (you might want to hold the mask over your face to get the position right). Knot the ends to secure and the mask is ready to wear.

TIP / Try using orange-brown and white papers to give the mask the look of a fox, or shades of silver-grey to turn it into a wolf.

GRAPH PAPER CROSS STITCH

YOU WILL NEED:

Graph paper pattern (from cut-out sheet)
Craft foam or old mouse mat
Small, sharp needle
Embroidery threads
Frame with picture mount (optional)

TIP / Look out for other cross stitch patterns and try working them on sheets of standard graph paper. Squared pages from maths exercise books would also work.

1 Place the graph paper pattern from the cut-out section on a piece of craft foam or old mouse mat and use a sharp needle to make small holes in the corners of each marked cross.

2 Cut a length of embroidery cotton and split it in half to work with three strands. Begin sewing over each cross marked on the paper. You can use a single colour, or work with multiple shades using the diagram as a guide.

3 Slip the finished design behind a picture mount ready to frame. Alternatively, to display as a freestanding piece, trim excess paper from around the edges as desired.

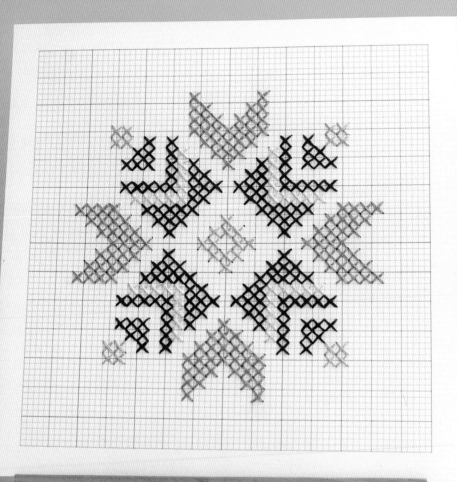

HALF-CUT CARDS

YOU WILL NEED:

Patterned card
Patterned paper
Glue stick
Craft knife

TECHNIQUE: Papercutting

1 Cut patterned card 16 x 14cm (6¼ x 5½in) for the snowflake or 18 x 15cm (7 x 6in) for the deer. Score and fold in half, with the pattern on the inside. Cut a contrasting piece of paper 8 x 14cm (3⅛ x 5½in) (snowflake) or 9 x 15cm (3½ x 6in) (deer). Glue to the front of the folded card.

2 Copy the snowflake or deer template onto a third piece of patterned paper and cut out. Fold the finished shape neatly in half and glue to the inside of the card, matching the fold lines. Place flat to allow the glue to dry.

3 Working on the left-hand side of the centre fold only, cut precisely around the edges of the original deer or snowflake, cutting through the layers of card and paper beneath.

4 Fold over the front of the card, so the cut-out detail stands away from the spine. To fit into an envelope, fold the cut-out section over so it sits snugly in the gap at the front of the card. It will pop out again when the card is opened.

TIP It's tricky to write your message inside a card like this, so add it to the back of the card instead – no one will mind when it's a greeting this smart!

STORAGE TINS

YOU WILL NEED:

Empty tin or container (e.g., a cocoa tin)
Patterned papers
Glue stick or spray adhesive
Label (optional)

1 Measure the height and circumference of your tin. Use the measurements to cut out a piece of paper, adding an extra 2cm (¾in) to the circumference to allow the ends to overlap.

2 Apply glue to the back of the paper and carefully wrap it around the tin, smoothing it down with your hands.

3 Cut a second, contrasting piece of paper the same size and stick this to the inside of the tin.

4 Add an optional label to decorate the front.

TIP / If the upper edge of your tin has a raw edge, add an extra 5cm (2in) to the height when you cut out the paper. Stick to the tin and cut vertical slits about 1cm (⅜in) apart in the excess paper. Spread glue around the tin's inside edge. Fold over each paper piece and press down onto the glue to create a neat, paper-covered edge.

PAPER CAMEO BROOCHES

YOU WILL NEED:

Profile photograph

Temporary or re-positionable spray adhesive

Black paper

Craft knife

Cameo frame

Patterned paper

Glass or domed-plastic cover (optional)

Brooch pin

PVA glue and glue stick

TECHNIQUE: Jewellery

1 To make a silhouette, find (or take) a photograph of your subject in profile. Print or photocopy it at a size to fit inside the cameo frame.

2 Use temporary adhesive to fix the image to a piece of black paper. Carefully cut around the outside with a craft knife. Peel off the original image and discard.

3 Cut an oval of patterned paper to fit inside the cameo frame. Glue the black paper silhouette to the patterned oval. Stick both into place inside the frame. Add an optional glass or domed plastic cover on top to seal the silhouette inside.

4 Squeeze a line of glue over the back of the brooch pin. Press it into place on the back of the frame, placing it about a third of the way down from the top edge. Allow the glue to dry completely before wearing.

TIP / Use the same technique to make a larger silhouette and display it in a picture frame instead – either in an oval-shaped frame or a standard rectangle.

STARRY TEALIGHT COVER

YOU WILL NEED:

Cover strip (see cut-out sheet)
Craft foam or old mouse mat
Sharp needle
PVA glue
Clothes pegs (clothespins)
Electric tealight

1 Snip the dark blue cover strip from the cut-out sheet, trimming just inside the edges so no white paper shows at all.

2 Place on a sheet of craft foam or old mouse mat and push a sharp needle down through each of the marked dots to make a hole.

3 Spread glue over one end of the strip, curve the other end round and press down onto it. Line up the pattern of holes for a neat finish. Hold the top and bottom edges together with clothes pegs as the glue dries.

4 Place the finished cover over an electric tealight. Alternatively, you could use a real candle as long as it's safely enclosed in a clear, heat-proof votive holder.

TIP / No craft foam? No problem – use a padded ironing board as your work surface instead.

TIP / Glass glitter is more expensive than the acrylic but definitely worth it as it reflects light beautifully and also ages to a lovely patina.

GLOBE LIGHT

YOU WILL NEED:

Basic party balloon
Glass or small bowl
Permanent marker pen
Tissue paper (white and silver)
Wallpaper paste
PVA glue
German glass glitter
Nylon thread
Sharp needle
Electric tealight

TECHNIQUE: Papier Mâché

1 Inflate a balloon with a couple of breaths, so it's small and round. Tie a knot in the end. Place a glass or small bowl over the knotted end and draw a circle around it with a permanent marker.

2 Tear tissue paper into small pieces. Spread a thin layer of wallpaper paste over the back of the first one and smooth down onto the balloon's surface. Add a second piece, slightly overlapping the first. Keep going to cover the balloon, leaving the area inside the marked circle clear. Add five or more layers to create a strong structure. Use silver tissue for the final layer.

3 When dry, spread PVA glue on a small area at a time. Sprinkle glitter over the glue, pat down gently and shake off excess. Repeat, to cover all the papier mâché with glitter. Allow to dry thoroughly.

4 Snip off the knot and pull the balloon out. Fold a length of thread in half and knot the ends together. Pierce a hole in the top of the globe with a needle. Take the thread up through it to make a hanger. Slip an electric tealight inside the globe to display.

BUTTONS + CUFF LINKS

YOU WILL NEED:

Flat or slightly domed buttons
(wooden or plastic)
Patterned paper
PVA glue or découpage medium
Emery board
Paper piercing tool
Varnish (optional)
Cuff-link blanks (optional)

TIP / The buttons shown here were all decorated with patterned paper cut from security envelopes.

1 Cut a piece of paper slightly larger than your button. Spread adhesive over the back and press firmly down on top of the button.

2 Leave to dry, then gently sand around the outside with an emery board to smooth out the join between the paper and the button.

3 Use a piercing tool to make holes in the paper, corresponding with each of the original buttonholes.

4 Brush on an optional coat of varnish to seal and protect the buttons.

5 To turn a pair of decorated buttons into cuff links, use strong adhesive to fix each one to the flat pad of a cuff-link blank.

Alternatives:

Glue patterned paper to the underside of transparent buttons, rather than on top.

Cut or punch out a circle and stick it to the centre of a larger button, leaving a border around the outside. This works especially well with buttons that have an indent in the centre.

BLUEPRINT STATIONERY

YOU WILL NEED:

Lightweight paper (e.g., old book pages, blueprints, origami paper or thin gift wrap)

Plain wooden pencils

Découpage medium

Binder clips

Glue stick

Plain white eraser

Wooden pencil sharpener

Wooden ruler

Small notebook (optional)

TECHNIQUE: Folding + Scoring

To decorate a pencil:

Cut a strip of paper the same length as the pencil body and wide enough to wrap around it with ends overlapping. Spread découpage medium on the back of the paper. Place the pencil against one long edge and roll it up so the paper wraps firmly around. Smooth out any wrinkles and set aside to dry.

To decorate a binder clip:

Cut a piece of paper the same width and long enough to fold around the binder clip. Snip off a narrow rectangle on both sides of the short ends, so the paper fits snugly into the clip mechanism. Spread glue over the back and smooth down onto the clip.

To decorate an eraser:

Cut a strip of paper slightly shorter than the eraser and long enough to wrap around it with about 1cm (⅜in) overlapping at the back. Glue the overlapped ends together.

To decorate a sharpener:

Do the same as for the eraser, but without the overlapped ends. Glue the patterned paper directly to the edges of the sharpener.

To decorate a ruler:

Glue a narrow strip of paper over the flat part of a ruler, close to the bottom (non-measuring) edge.

TIP / Decorate a notebook with scraps of leftover paper to match the rest of the stationery set.

TIP / Try to pick napkins that have a similar background colour to your painted jar, so the edges of the cut-out shapes blend seamlessly into the shade beneath.

FLOWER JARS

YOU WILL NEED:

Glass jar
Spray paint
Scissors
Paper napkins
Découpage medium

TECHNIQUE: Découpage

1 Wash the jar. When completely dry, cover the outside with three to four coats of spray paint in a light, neutral colour. Set aside to dry.

2 Using a small, sharp pair of scissors, cut out the motifs you want to use from the paper napkins. Leave a very narrow border around the edges so the motif outline stands out clearly. When you've finished cutting, peel away the lower layers of the napkin, to leave just the very thin, coloured top layer.

3 Brush a thin layer of découpage medium over a small section of the jar. Carefully press one of the cut-out motifs down on top of it and smooth out with your fingers. Add the remaining motifs to build up a pattern.

4 Allow the découpage medium to dry and then brush on two to three additional coats to seal and protect the surface.

YOU'RE-A-STAR SHAKER CARD

YOU WILL NEED:

Thick card e.g., mountboard
Patterned papers
Clear acetate (see Tip)
Square card blank
Glue stick
Shaker filling, e.g., wood veneer
shapes, sequins or tiny beads
Alphabet stickers

1 Copy the red and blue lines from the circle template onto thick card and cut out to make a ring shape. Repeat, cutting two more rings from patterned paper. Copy the red line onto clear acetate twice, and cut two identical circles. Copy the black line onto the front of the card blank and cut out to create an aperture.

2 Spread glue around the aperture edges on the inside of the card. Press one of the acetate circles onto the glue and stick a patterned-paper ring over the acetate edges. Add glue to one side of the cardboard ring and press the second acetate circle on top. Stick a patterned paper ring over the acetate.

3 Sprinkle your filling into the centre of the first acetate circle. Spread glue over the back of the card ring and press down onto the card. The filling should be securely sandwiched between the two layers, but free to move around when you shake the card.

4 Glue a contrasting piece of patterned paper to the inside back of the card. Use alphabet stickers to add a message to the front.

TIP / You can buy sheets of acetate from craft shops and stationery stores, or try recycling clear plastic lids instead (e.g., from soft cheese or yoghurt containers).

MAKE-AN-IMPRESSION WALL HANGING

YOU WILL NEED:

Thick watercolour paper or
medium-weight card
Craft knife
Lightbox (optional – see Tip)
Washi or masking tape
Smooth, lightweight watercolour
paper or cartridge paper 27 x 37cm
(10½ x 14½in)
Embossing stylus

TECHNIQUE: Papercutting

1 Copy the main template onto thick watercolour paper. Use a craft knife to cut away the areas inside the outline, creating a stencil. Tape this to a window or lightbox. Tape a sheet of lightweight watercolour paper on top. Trace around the edges of the stencil with an embossing stylus, using a firm, even pressure. Lift off the top sheet.

2 Copy the detail sections onto thick watercolour paper and cut out. Tape to a window and, using the diagram as a guide, reposition the top sheet, so the detail sits in the relevant part of the design. Lightly shade the design edges in pencil on the back of the paper, so they're easier to see.

3 Emboss the detailed sections one at a time. You only need to cut out details like the flower centres once and then move the top sheet around to retrace the shape in different places.

4 Display in a wooden skirt hanger, decorating with a strip of patterned paper if desired.

 TIP/ You only need a lightbox to complete this project if you're working after dark. During the day, a window works perfectly (and is cost-free!).

TEN-MINUTE BANNER CARDS

YOU WILL NEED:

Cut-out patterned cards (or see Tip)
Corner-rounder punch (optional)
Plain white card
Alphabet stickers or old books
and magazines
Glue stick

1 Cut out your chosen card from the cut-out sheet at the back of the book. Score along the join between the plain and patterned sections and then fold in half. Use a corner-rounder to trim all four corners, or leave them square.

2 Cut a 1.5 x 14.5cm (⅝ x 5¾in) strip of paper for a landscape (horizontal) card, or a 1.5 x 10.5cm (⅝ x 4¼in) strip if it's portrait (vertical).

3 Snip a V shape into each end of the strip and then fold it as shown in the diagram to form a banner. Gently curl the ends of the strip around a pencil so they flick upwards.

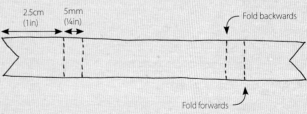

4 Use alphabet stickers or words and letters cut from an old book to spell out a message.

5 Add a small amount of glue to the back of the strip and then press into place on the front of the card.

TIP / Use this idea to make cards with whatever supplies you have to hand. Fold a piece of patterned card in half, or use a plain piece covered with gift wrap, book text, doodles, a page from a glossy magazine, or a printable pattern from an online design store. Add a banner with a message, and you're done.

WOODEN BEAD NECKLACE

YOU WILL NEED:

Plain or patterned papers
Wooden beads (plain and coloured)
Découpage medium
Leather thong or cord

TECHNIQUE: Découpage + Jewellery

TIP / Choose papers that are as thin as possible. Tissue works well, as do pages torn from unwanted books, magazines or clothing catalogues.

1 Tear the paper into tiny pieces – as a rough guide, and depending on the size of your beads, the pieces should be no bigger than 1 x 1.5cm (⅜ x ⅝in).

2 Spread découpage medium over the back of the first piece and place it onto the bead. Press down firmly, smooth over the edges and make sure it's as flat as possible.

3 Add a second piece in the same way, overlapping the first. Keep going, adding one piece at a time until the whole bead is covered.

4 When the découpage medium is completely dry, brush on one to two additional coats to seal and protect the finished bead.

5 Thread the paper-decorated beads onto a length of thong or cord, adding a few solid coloured beads in amongst them for variety.

DIY STAMPS

YOU WILL NEED:

Plain, flat eraser
Craft knife
Lino cutting tool (optional)
Ink and surfaces for stamping
(e.g., card)

TECHNIQUE: Stamping + Embossing

1 Copy the flower template onto the surface of an eraser in pencil. Using a craft knife, cut around the outline. Don't cut through the full depth – just a few millimetres. Make more cuts from the flower outline to the edges of the eraser, dividing the space around the design into small sections. Then, working from the side edges, slice horizontally across the eraser towards the flower's edges. Lift away each section as you cut. The finished design should be raised above the remaining parts of the eraser.

2 You can leave the flower as an outline shape, adding the centre circle with a cut out piece of paper, or use a fine lino cutter to carve out the circle. To do this, draw a circle onto the eraser, then 'trace' over the line with the tool. The V-shaped blade will scoop out a continuous piece of the eraser as you move it around. Use a chunkier blade to scoop and carve away the area inside the circular outline, taking away a depth of several millimetres.

3 Ink up the finished stamp and use to make cards, gift wrap or simple pictures.

Alternative:

For an extra-quick alternative, turn the round eraser at the end of a pencil into a simple heart shape by making a few cuts with a craft knife.

FOLDED CARD HOLDER

} Thin card (plain or patterned)
Glue stick
Patterned paper (optional) {

TECHNIQUE: Folding + Scoring

TIP / You can adjust the size of the template to hold larger cards, photos, invitations or gift vouchers.

1 Copy the holder template onto thin card. Cut out, then score and fold along the dotted lines, as marked.

2 With the right side of the card facing down, fold the bottom strip (A) up over section B. Fold over section C to lie on top of them. Spread glue over pieces A and C and fold over section D, pressing down firmly.

3 Finish off the basic structure with decorative details (optional). To add a contrasting pattern inside the holder, cut an 8 x 5.7cm (3 x 2¼in) rectangle of paper. Spread glue over the back and slip inside the card holder. Line up the top corners, before pressing firmly into position.

4 Cut or punch a 2cm (¾in) circle of paper in a contrasting pattern and glue to the diagonal edge of the card holder. Alternatively, wrap a narrow strip of paper around the holder, just above the bottom edge, and overlap the ends to fix in place.

5 Use the holder to make your business cards look extra-impressive, as an alternative way to present a gift card, or to hold save-the-date cards for a wedding celebration.

A LITTLE BIRDHOUSE FOR YOUR SOUL

YOU WILL NEED:

Small cardboard box (e.g., empty teabag container)
Craft knife
Glue stick
Patterned paper and thin card
Piercing tool or large needle
Painted dowel stick

TECHNIQUE: Folding + Scoring

1 Mark a dot at the centre top edge of the box. Measure 6cm (2⅜in) down from each top corner and mark two more dots. Join the side dots to the centre one, creating two diagonal lines. Score along each one. Repeat on the back of the box.

2 Cut the front and back flaps off the top of the box. Slice down into each corner edge from the top to the 6cm (2⅜in) mark (see diagram). Fold along the scored lines. Fold the sides of the box in towards the centre and glue to the folded-over edges (A and B). Trim excess from the apex of the house.

3 Cover the front, back and side edges with patterned paper. Draw a circle onto the front of the box and cut out. Cut a strip of thin card, large enough to fold over the slanting roof edges, plus 1cm (⅜in) border on all sides. Cover with patterned paper, fold in half and glue into place for the roof.

4 Use a piercing tool to make holes in the front and back of the house, about 4cm (1½in) up from the bottom. Push a painted dowel stick through the holes as a perch.

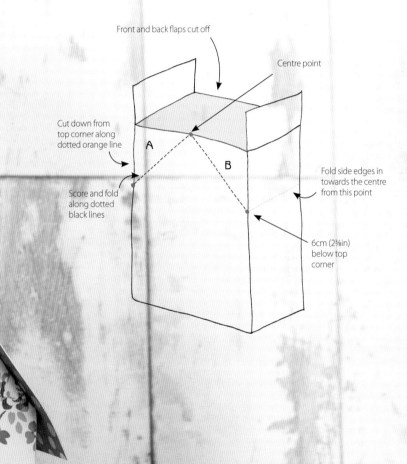

Front and back flaps cut off

Centre point

Cut down from top corner along dotted orange line

Score and fold along dotted black lines

A

B

Fold side edges in towards the centre from this point

6cm (2⅜in) below top corner

TIP / The measurements given are for a box roughly 9 x 16cm (3½ x 6¼in). You may need to adjust them if using a box that is much larger or smaller.

PAPER-PIECED PORTRAIT

YOU WILL NEED:

Flesh-toned card or paper
Glue stick
Fine black marker pen
Selection of papers (plain or patterned)
Picture frame

TECHNIQUE: Collage

1 Copy the head template onto flesh-toned card or paper twice and cut out. Trim the ears off one piece and glue this on top of the other one. Draw on facial features with a fine marker pen. Cut two circles of paper to make cheeks and glue into position.

2 Cut the two hair pieces and moustache from plain or patterned paper in a hair colour of your choice. Glue the smaller hair piece on top of the large one and stick to the head. Add the moustache between the nose and mouth.

3 Cut out the clothes – shirt, collar, tie, tie knot and sweater – from patterned papers. Glue the knot to the top of the tie and fix both to the neck of the shirt. Add the collar on top, allowing the ends to flip upwards slightly. Stick the tank top between the shirt and the tie. Glue the clothing piece to the body.

4 Cut a piece of paper to fit inside your frame (a rectangle or square would work just as well as the oval one shown), and stick the finished figure on top.

TIP/ If your frame has a ridge or lip around the inside edge, try covering it with tiny scraps of paper to complement the finished portrait.

GO-FOR-GOLD NOTEBOOKS

YOU WILL NEED:

Double-sided adhesive sheet
Notebook
Gold leaf
Soft brush and stiff brush
Patterned paper
Glue stick

To make the flower notebook:

1 Trace the flower template onto the double-sided adhesive sheet. Cut out and peel away the backing paper. Press the sticky side down onto the notebook. Rub over the top to ensure it is well adhered. Peel away the top sheet.

2 Place a sheet of gold leaf gently on top. Tap it into place with a soft brush, so you see the flower outline showing through the leaf.

3 When the design is covered, rub around the flower edges with a stiffer brush. The leaf will break away in areas where it's not stuck down. Set aside larger pieces to re-use later and rub around the outline again to remove smaller bits and create a neat, sharp edge.

To make the geometric notebook:

1 Copy the geometric template onto the adhesive sheet, cut out and remove backing. Cut pieces of patterned paper to fit behind several of the triangular gaps and press onto the back of the adhesive.

2 Add a little glue to the back of the paper triangles and press the whole thing into place on the front of the notebook.

3 Peel off the top sheet and gild, as described for the flower.

GEOMETRIC JEWELLERY

YOU WILL NEED:

Thick card
White or cream acrylic paint
Small brush
Patterned papers
PVA glue
Needle or paper piercing tool
Jump rings
Necklace chain and clasp

TECHNIQUE: Jewellery

1 Copy your chosen template (circles or triangles) onto thick card and use a craft knife to cut out the pieces.

2 Brush two coats of white or cream paint over the side and back edges of the card.

3 Cut out patterned paper pieces to fit on top of each card section and glue firmly in place. Allow to dry. Stick the covered card pieces together – the single triangle on top of the double triangle, or the full circle on top of the partial circle.

4 Use a needle or paper piercing tool to make a small hole at each side of the necklace, as marked on the template.

5 Open out two jump rings and thread one through each of the holes. Slip a length of chain onto each ring before squeezing them shut again. Add a clasp to the opposite end of the chain and your necklace is ready to wear.

TIP / For a glossy finish, or to make the necklace more hard-wearing, brush on one to two coats of clear varnish.

BEST-DRESSED EGG CUPS

TECHNIQUE: Papier Mâché

1 Cut the top off the bottle and turn it upside down to check an egg fits comfortably inside. Remove the lid and discard.

2 Spread glue around the inside of the bottle neck. Stuff newspaper inside the neck, pressing down firmly so the end is level.

3 Cut out a card circle and glue the bottle neck in the centre to form an egg cup shape.

4 Cover the whole thing with four or five layers of papier mâché. Allow to dry thoroughly before brushing on two coats of white paint.

To make the floral egg cup:

1 Tear decorative tissue into small pieces and paste on over the dry, painted surface. When the tissue is dry, brush on two coats of clear varnish.

2 Cut out a bow shape from patterned paper. Cover both sides with sticky tape, trimming away excess around the edges. Add a little glue to the centre back, and press into place at the top edge of the egg cup.

To make the stripy egg cup:

1 Paint bands of colour around the top section with a fine brush.

2 Add two coats of clear varnish, once the painted stripes are dry. Finish off by gluing on two small buttons.

TIP / Obviously, paper egg cups shouldn't be immersed in water, but the varnished finish means you can wipe them clean with a warm, soapy sponge after use.

FAUX LETTERPRESS POSTER

YOU WILL NEED:

Red and blue vellum (or alternative colours of your choice)

Double-sided adhesive sheet

Smooth watercolour paper or poster board

Scrap paper

Washi or masking tape

40 x 50cm (15¾ x 19¾in) frame with picture mount

1 Trace the template letters – three each of L, V and E, plus six Os – onto red and blue vellum and press onto one side of a double-sided adhesive sheet. Cut out, snipping just inside the traced lines.

2 Cut a 40 x 50cm (15¾ x 19¾in) piece of watercolour paper for the background, plus a strip of scrap paper, the same width, with one long edge perfectly straight. Tape the strip ends to the background, about a third of the way down from the top edge.

3 Peel the protective sheet off one adhesive-backed vellum L. Starting just left of centre, press it onto the background, aligning the bottom with the paper strip's straight edge. Add an O in the same way, slightly overlapping the L, and then a second O, overlapping the first. Stick down V and E in the same way. Remove the paper strip. Measure 8.5cm (3⅜in) down from the bottom of the letters and replace the strip to mark a new baseline.

4 Repeat step 3 to add the second and third 'LOVE'. Use a ruler to line up the vertical edges of the Ls. Frame the finished poster.

TIP/ If you can't find the right vellum colours, make custom shades by printing large blocks or rectangles onto a sheet of good quality tracing paper instead.

SNACK JARS

YOU WILL NEED:

Glass jar with lid
White spray paint
Patterned tissue paper
Découpage medium

1 Wash the jar, including lid, and allow to dry thoroughly. Cover the lid with three to four coats of white spray paint. Set aside to dry.

2 Cut a circle of tissue 3–4cm (1¼–1½in) bigger all round than the lid. Spread découpage medium over the upper surface of the lid and press the tissue down on top, smoothing out any wrinkles with your fingers.

3 Make slits roughly 1cm (⅜in) apart in the excess tissue around the edges. Spread découpage medium onto the edges of the lid, inside and out. Fold each paper piece down over the side of the lid and tuck the ends neatly inside. Add extra medium to stick in place, if needed.

4 Allow to dry. Brush on one to two extra coats of découpage medium or non-toxic varnish to seal and protect the decorated lid.

TECHNIQUE: Découpage

TIP / Decorate similar jars to use for different purposes around the home – maybe bath salts in the bathroom, loose change in the hallway or paperclips in the study.

VINTAGE SLIDE-REEL CARD

YOU WILL NEED:

Old View-Master slide reel
Craft knife
Tiny photographs
Printed initials and icons or alphabet
and shape stickers
Patterned papers
PVA glue
Cocktail stick or toothpick
Letter or word stickers

1 Slip a craft knife carefully between the layers of the slide reel to prise them apart. Move it all the way around, gently separating the outer edges (don't worry about opening up the circular, inner section). Pull out the film slides and discard.

2 Measure the holes in the slides and cut out photos, initials, simple icons (e.g., hearts and stars) and scraps of patterned paper to fit inside. Allow a border of a few millimetres around the outside of each piece.

3 Use a cocktail stick or toothpick to apply a thin layer of glue around the inner edges of each aperture. Slip a piece of paper into place behind each opening. Now add more glue to the inside surfaces of the reel. Press down firmly to join the front and back sections, sandwiching your new images between.

4 Glue a circle of patterned paper over the centre of the reel and use alphabet stickers to spell out a message or sentiment. Write your chosen wedding or anniversary greeting in the space on the back of the reel.

TIP/ Fold a smart, square envelope from coordinating patterned paper or gift wrap to hold the card.

MAKE-A-SPECTACLE GLASSES

YOU WILL NEED:
Glasses or sunglasses
Emery board
Thin paper or tissue
Découpage medium

TECHNIQUE: Découpage

1 Use an emery board to gently sand the arms of your glasses on the flat, outer surface only (to help the paper adhere more firmly). Cut a piece of paper that's larger all round than the arm you're covering. Accuracy isn't important, but make sure one of the short ends is cut in a neat, straight line.

2 Spread découpage medium over the flat outer surface of the first arm and down onto the sides of the arm. Press the paper on top, lining up the straight edge with the straight, hinged end of the arm. Smooth it out with your fingers, but don't press it down onto the side edges of the arm. Repeat with the other arm and leave to dry.

3 To remove excess paper, and create a smooth, flush join between the paper and the glasses, gently sand along the edges of the arm.with the emery board. The excess paper will start to break away and the dried medium will stop the emery board scratching the plastic. Rub away any excess medium with a baby wipe. Brush on two extra coats of découpage medium to seal and protect the decorated arms.

PAJAKI CHANDELIER

YOU WILL NEED:

Wooden embroidery hoop 18cm (7in)
Washi tape (two contrasting patterns)
Paper straws
Plain or patterned tissue paper
Fine nylon thread (e.g., beading thread)
Small metal ring
Wooden bead
Needle
Thin paper and scraps of
patterned paper
Glue stick
Six clear buttons

1 Separate an embroidery hoop and discard the outer section. Press a strip of washi tape into place around the outside edge of the inner hoop. Add contrasting tape to the inside edge.

2 Cut the paper straws into 57 lengths, each 4cm (1½in). Punch or cut out 126 circles of tissue paper.

3 Cut three 80cm (31in) lengths of thread and loop through a metal ring. Fold the threads in half (ring in the middle) with six equal thread lengths hanging below. Slide a wooden bead over all six strands and knot.

4 Take one of the strands and use a needle to thread on a piece of straw, followed by three tissue circles. Repeat four more times and add one more straw. Tie the thread around the hoop to hold straws and circles in position. Repeat with the rest of the threads, spacing the knotted ends evenly around the hoop.

5 Cut 40cm (16in) of thread. Tie one end next to the knotted end of one of the upper strands, thread on a straw and three tissue circles. Repeat, and add three more straws. Finish off with three tissue circles, a straw, three circles and a straw. Tie the end to the hoop, opposite the starting point. Repeat, adding two more loops to the bottom of the chandelier.

6 Make six paper flowers (as described in the Blossoms + Branch project). Glue a circle of paper to the centre of each one and add a clear button on top. Stitch through the button, taking the threads twice around the hoop to attach a flower to the bottom of each decorated strand. Snip all excess threads to finish.

TIP / For a speedy alternative, use store-bought paper flowers to decorate the paper chandelier, instead of folding your own from scratch.

POSABLE PAPER DOLLS

YOU WILL NEED:

Girl and boy cut-out figures
Craft knife or needle
Mini brads (paper fasteners), in
various colours

1 Cut out each of the pieces from the cut-out sheet at the back of the book.

2 Use the point of a craft knife or a needle to make holes in each one, as marked.

3 Push a small brad through the holes to join the pieces together, e.g. through the top left of the girl's dress and then through the top of the left upper arm. Bend the legs of the brad open to hold it in place.

4 When you've joined all the pieces together, move and pose each figure as you like. You could stick a magnet to the back of each figure so you can display (and pose) the dolls on your fridge, or fix them to a cork noticeboard using a single map pin towards the top of the body.

TIP / The girl figure has three leg pieces on the cut-out sheet, but you'll obviously only need two. You can pick whether she has walking legs (both feet facing in the same direction) or standing legs (feet pointing in opposite directions).

STICKY TAPE TRANSFERS

YOU WILL NEED:

Picture, pattern or photograph
Clear, wide parcel tape
Glass bottles, jars or containers
Metal spoon
Bowl of water

1 Find or print out an image to fit on the front of your glass container and photocopy it (see Tip).

2 Cut a piece of tape and carefully press it down over the photocopied image. Try to keep it straight and avoid wrinkles or air bubbles in the tape. Rub firmly all over the surface of the tape with the back of a metal spoon to make sure it's fully adhered.

3 Submerge the tape in a bowl of water for about a minute and then start rubbing the paper with your fingers. It should begin to lift away from the tape, leaving just the ink image behind.

4 When you've completely removed all traces of paper, press the transfer into place on a glass container or bottle. There should be enough stickiness left in the tape for it to adhere.

TIP / This technique won't work with copies made on an inkjet printer. You need to use a large copier (the kind found in offices or your local library), which uses toner rather than ink cartridges.

ANY-OCCASION CRACKERS

YOU WILL NEED:

Thin white card
Cardboard tube
Cracker snap
Double-sided tape
White thread
Patterned paper
Decorations, e.g., chipboard hearts, wooden initials (optional)

TECHNIQUE: Scoring + Folding

1 Using the diagram as a guide, cut out a rectangle of thin card. Score and fold along the dotted lines, then smooth the card flat again.

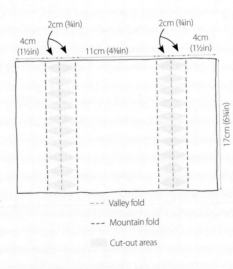

2cm (¾in) 4cm (1½in) 11cm (4⅜in) 2cm (¾in) 4cm (1½in)

17cm (6¾in)

--- Valley fold

--- Mountain fold

▓▓▓ Cut-out areas

2 To cut out the diamond-shaped sections, re-fold along the red lines and snip out triangles, cutting through both layers of the folded card. Do this at each end.

3 Place a cracker snap near one edge of the card and wrap the centre section tightly around a cardboard tube. Stick the edges of the card together where they overlap, with the snap sandwiched between card and tube.

4 Tie thread around the cut-out section at one end. Pull taut, knot the ends together and snip off excess thread. Fill the cracker from the opposite end and then tie that shut.

5 Cut patterned paper 17 x 11cm (6¾in x 4½in) and wrap around the cracker centre. Overlap the ends and glue into place. Stick decorations to the front of the cracker.

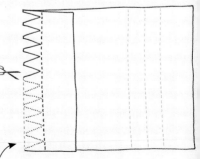

Cut out triangles between the orange and black fold lines

DIAMOND PIÑATA

YOU WILL NEED:

Medium-weight card or
watercolour paper
PVA glue
Washi or masking tape
Large confetti in white and various
colours (to make your own – see
Custom Confetti project)
Sharp needle
Fine string or nylon thread

☆

1 Copy the triangle and tab templates onto card and cut out. Trace around them onto a larger sheet, as shown. Cut around the outer edge, score and then fold along the inner lines, as marked. Spread glue over the tabs and fold the diamond into shape, sticking each tab behind the corresponding straight edge. Use strips of masking tape to hold the edges together as the glue dries.

2 Remove the tape and spread glue over one face of the diamond. Sprinkle white confetti over the glue and press down, overlapping the pieces to create a fluffy effect. Allow the glue to dry. Repeat on each face in turn until the whole diamond is covered.

3 Arrange ten or more extra pieces of coloured confetti on each face, sticking them down individually with a dot of glue.

4 Use a needle to poke two holes at the apex of the diamond. Cut a length of fine string and thread it through the holes. Knot the ends together to make a hanging loop.

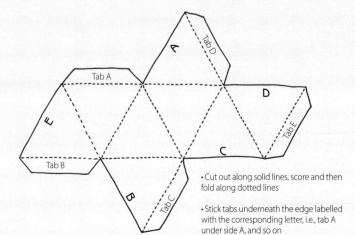

• Cut out along solid lines, score and then fold along dotted lines

• Stick tabs underneath the edge labelled with the corresponding letter, i.e., tab A under side A, and so on

ALPINE
MOBILE

YOU WILL NEED:

Alpine cut-outs
Garden stick or chunky twig
Fine nylon thread
Glue stick

1 Cut out each of the pieces from the cut-out sheet at the back of the book, trimming just outside the outlined edge.

2 To make the hanger, cut a piece of clean, dry stick or twig 20–25cm (8–10in) long. Cut about 12cm (4¾in) of nylon thread and tie one end around the stick centre. Spread glue over the back of the sun/front piece and press the opposite end of the thread down on top, in the centre. Press the sun/back piece on top, to sandwich the thread between the suns.

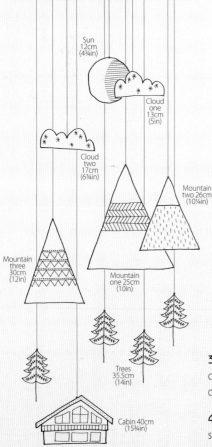

Sun
12cm
(4¾in)

Cloud
one
13cm
(5in)

Cloud
two
17cm
(6¾in)

Mountain
two 26cm
(10¼in)

Mountain
three
30cm
(12in)

Mountain
one 25cm
(10in)

Trees
35.5cm
(14in)

Cabin 40cm
(15¾in)

3 Repeat with the cloud one pieces, overlapping the ends onto the sun. Add the rest of the pieces in order, using the diagram as a guide, and staggering the thread lengths.

4 Cut 50cm (20in) of thread for a hanger (or longer or shorter as desired). Tie one thread end to each end of the stick, trimming away excess thread from the knot tails.

TIP / You can either hang the finished mobile flat against a wall, or, because the double-sided pieces look the same from font and back, suspend it from the ceiling.

FANCY STICKING PLASTERS

YOU WILL NEED:

White or translucent plasters
(adhesive bandages)
Patterned tissue paper
Gel medium
Thin card
Patterned paper
Glue stick

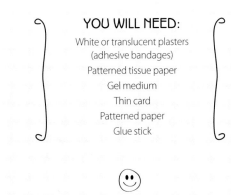

TECHNIQUE: Folding + Scoring, Découpage

To make the plasters:

Cut a piece of patterned tissue slightly larger than your first plaster. Brush a thin layer of gel medium over the front of the plaster and press the tissue down on top. Leave to dry. Trim away excess tissue around the edges. Repeat to make as many plasters as you like.

To make the box:

1 Copy the box template onto thin card and cut out. Score and then fold along the dotted lines, as marked.

2 Stick tab E under section A and then fold the smaller tabs (F) towards the centre of the box. Glue section G on top and section H on top of that, forming the base of the box. Fold the two J pieces inwards and then stick the two K pieces to the underside of section L. This forms the box lid.

3 Cut a cross shape from patterned paper and glue to the front of the box to decorate. Slip your plasters inside.

TIP You can use traditional flesh-toned plasters for this project, but bear in mind the colour may show through your tissue, altering the way it looks.

FOLDED PAPER BAG

TECHNIQUE: Folding + Scoring

1 Cut a piece of paper large enough to wrap around the box. Score, fold over 1–2cm (⅜–¾in) at the top edge and stick down to create a narrow 'hem'. Repeat at one of the side edges.

2 Wrap the paper around the sides of the box, pressing neat, firm creases at each corner. The ends should overlap by 2–3cm (¾–1¼in). Stick them together with the hemmed end on top.

TIP / The width and depth of the box used determines the measurements of your finished bag. The height can be adjusted; for instance, to make a shorter bag, just wrap the bottom half of the box. The box is only used to form the bag – it won't be altered in any way.

3 Fold over the paper ends at the base of the box, as if wrapping a normal parcel and stick in place (see diagram).

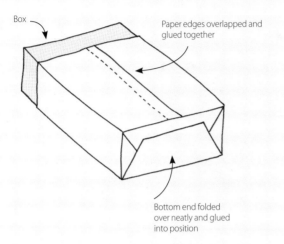

Box

Paper edges overlapped and glued together

Bottom end folded over neatly and glued into position

4 Carefully slide the box out of your newly formed bag. Draw around the base onto a piece of cardboard. Cut out the card and glue inside the bottom of the bag.

5 At the top of the bag, take the front right-hand corner and the back right-hand corner between your thumb and forefinger. Pinch together so the right-hand side of the bag folds to the inside (see diagram). Gently press along the side to form a crease. Repeat on the left side.

6 Punch two holes near the top of the bag. Tie a knot in the end of your ribbon, string or cord and feed through one of the holes from the inside out. Go back through the opposite hole and tie another knot to secure. (You can make the handle as long or short as you like.) Repeat on the other side of the bag to finish.

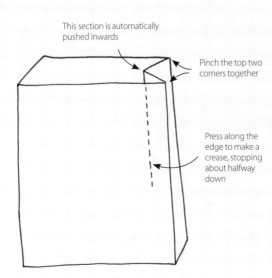

This section is automatically pushed inwards

Pinch the top two corners together

Press along the edge to make a crease, stopping about halfway down

Alternative:

For a sachet-style bag, follow steps 1–6. Now cut a piece of card, the same width as the bag, to make a fold-over flap. Score and fold, around 5cm (2in) from the bottom edge. Stick the section below the fold to the back of the bag, allowing the top part to fold over onto the front. Stitch a button to the front, so the flap can be slipped behind it to keep the bag closed.

TIP / You can use a mixture of papers (as shown here) or make your bracelet from a single print for a more uniform look.

PAPER LINKS BRACELET

YOU WILL NEED:

Thin patterned papers
Needle
Jump rings
Jewellery clasp

TECHNIQUE: Jewellery

1 Measure and cut out 20–25 strips of paper, each 4–9.5cm (1½–3¾in). Fold each one to make a link, as follows:

a) Fold the strip in half vertically. Press along the fold to mark a crease. Flatten the strip out and then fold both long edges in to meet the centre crease.

b) Fold the strip in half along the centre crease again, so the original cut edges are hidden inside.

c) Fold the strip in half widthways. Press along the fold to mark a crease. Undo the fold you made in the previous step and bring both short ends in to meet the centre crease.

d) Fold the strip in half widthways again, along the crease made in step c.

e) Pick up one of the links and you'll see the ends look like two flat loops. Take a second strip and push one end through each of these loops.

2 Push one end of a third link through each of the loops in the second link. Keep slotting the pieces together, building up a chevron pattern, until the bracelet fits your wrist.

3 Pierce a hole with a needle in the link at one end of the chain. Open out a jump ring and thread it through the hole. Add a clasp to the ring and squeeze it shut. Add the other part of the clasp to the opposite end to finish.

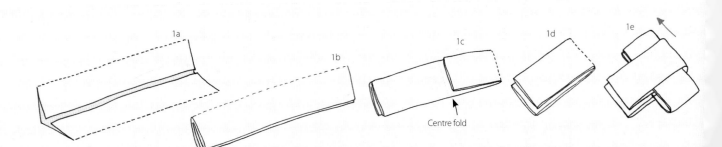

1a   1b   1c   Centre fold   1d   1e

TIP / If you can't find the perfect shade of night-sky blue for your banner, paint a sheet of plain white watercolour paper instead.

NIGHT SKY BANNER

YOU WILL NEED:

Navy blue card (see Tip)
Wooden dowel stick 8–10mm
(⁵⁄₁₆–³⁄₈in) diameter
Two metal eyelets or cup hooks
PVA glue
Clothes pegs (clothespins)
Small wood-veneer or paper stars
Needle and white thread
String or yarn

TECHNIQUE: Sewing on Paper

1 Cut out a 25 x 50cm (10 x 20in) piece of card. Mark a pencil line 8cm (3⅛in) above the bottom edge. Measure to find the centre point and draw diagonal lines down to each bottom corner. Cut along the lines to make a V-shaped fork.

2 Cut a 26.5cm (10½in) length of dowel and screw an eyelet or cup hook into each end. Spread glue over the back of the card, covering a strip about 5cm (2in) wide from the top edge down. Place the dowel onto the sticky card, with even amounts overlapping the sides, and tightly wrap the card around the stick. Hold in place with clothes pegs as the glue dries.

3 Glue stars to the banner to form constellations. You can base these on real ones or invent your own. Allow to dry. Stitch lines of running stitch between the stars, marking out the constellation patterns. Add extra stars in between to fill out the night sky.

4 Tie a length of string to the hooks at the end of the dowel and it's ready to hang.

BLOSSOMS + BRANCH

YOU WILL NEED:

Thin paper (two or three pale shades,
plus navy blue or black)
PVA glue
Cocktail stick
Small branch or twig
Washi or masking tape
White acrylic paint
Small paintbrush
Needle and thread
Herb or shredding scissors

TECHNIQUE: Papier Mâché

1 For each blossom, cut four identical flowers using either the medium or large template. Spread glue over the centre of one flower and press a second down on top, so the petals sit over the gaps between the petals of the flower below. Repeat with the second pair of flowers.

2 Take one of the pairs and gently pull the petals from the bottom flower up through the gaps in the top flower. Then, pull the petals from the top flower down through the gaps in the bottom one. Roll each petal around a cocktail stick, so it curls up and in towards the centre.

3 Repeat with the second pair of flowers, but this time curl the bottom layer of petals down. Spread glue over the centre and stick the first pair of flowers on top of the second. Make a selection of flowers in a mixture of colours and sizes.

4 Wrap narrow strips of tape around the bottom part(s) of the twig. Brush one or two coats of white paint in between the layers, creating stripes, and then carefully peel off the tape. Use a needle and thread to attach each flower to the twig (as if you were sewing on a button).

5 Use herb scissors to trim a fringe in the dark-coloured paper. Make perpendicular cuts across the fringe with the same scissors to create a pile of tiny square-shaped pieces. Squeeze a fairly thick layer of PVA into the centre of each flower, sprinkle the paper pieces on top and press down gently. Allow the glue to dry. Shake off any excess pieces.

TIP/ Standard printer or copier paper is the perfect weight for making these flowers. Try printing blocks of your chosen shade on both sides of a sheet to make custom-coloured petals.

SCREEN-PRINTED MATS

YOU WILL NEED:

Embroidery hoop 20cm (8in) diameter
Voile or sheer fabric
Découpage medium
Small paintbrush
Patterned paper
Acrylic paint
Screen-printing medium
A plastic card (e.g., old credit card)
Round, cork table mat (painted or plain)

1 Stretch voile or sheer fabric into the embroidery hoop and trim excess from the edges. Trace the apple template onto the fabric in pencil.

2 Using a small brush, fill in all the negative space (the white areas on the template) with découpage medium. Apply it fairly thickly, as though you were painting, and take it all the way out to the edges of the hoop frame. Leave to dry, and then brush on a second coat in the same way.

TIP / Screen-printing medium slows down paint drying time, making it easier to wash screens after use. If you don't plan to re-use your screen, omit the medium and just use paint.

3 When the screen is completely dry, place patterned paper on a flat, wipe-clean surface, taping down the edges to stop it moving. Place the screen on top, so the voile is directly against the paper.

4 Mix equal parts of paint and screen-printing medium in a small container. Add several blobs to your screen, just above the apple image, and stretching all along the width.

5 Hold the screen firmly in place with one hand. With the other hand, spread the paint mixture across the image, using a plastic card. Go over the whole image two or three times, making sure to keep the screen still. Set the card aside and very carefully lift the screen away from your paper.

6 When the printed image is dry, cut out a circle the same size as your cork mat, making sure the image sits in the centre. Spread découpage medium over the back of the paper and smooth it down firmly onto the top of the mat. Brush two to three extra coats of découpage medium on top to seal and protect.

Alternative:

Instead of making table place mats, you could use the same technique to print onto notebooks, cards, gift wrap, or to create simple pieces of wall art.

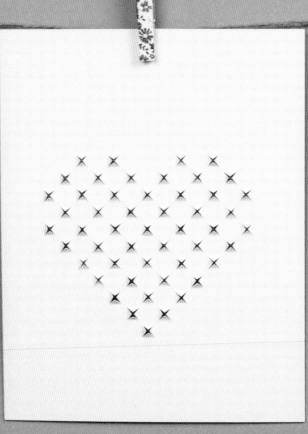

GEOMETRIC PAPERCUTS

Thin white or pale-coloured card
Coloured card
Craft knife
Clothes peg (clothespin) – optional

1 Trace the template onto the reverse of your card, marking each cross lightly in pencil.

2 Using a craft knife, carefully cut over each X using just two straight strokes. Now take a pencil and push the non-sharpened end through the centre of each cross, going from the back of the paper through to the front. Move it around in a gentle, circular motion to open out the X-shaped cut. Repeat with each of the crosses in turn.

3 To display, place a piece of coloured card behind the white sheet, trimming them both to the same size. Slip them into a frame. For a simpler option clip them together using a pretty clothes peg and hang on a display wire or length of string.

TIP / Experiment with creating different shapes and designs made up of the same cut-out X shapes. Simple cross stitch patterns are a terrific source of inspiration.

PAPER STRAW HIMMELI

YOU WILL NEED:
Six or seven paper straws (about 20cm/8in long)
Waxed thread

TIP / To make an asymmetrical himmeli, like the blue and white version shown, cut your straws into non-equal lengths instead of halves – for instance, a third/two-thirds.

1 Cut four paper straws in half and then cut four extra 6cm (2⅜in) lengths of straw. Snip a 1.8m (2yd) piece of waxed thread. Feed the thread through four half straws. Leaving a 20cm (8in) tail, make a knot in the thread so the straws form a closed diamond shape.

2 Slide two more half straws onto the thread and tie another knot at the bottom of the diamond. Add the last two half straws and knot the thread at the top.

3 Take the thread back down through one of the half straws to one of the centre joints in the structure. Feed it through a 6cm (2⅜in) length of straw and then wrap tightly around the next centre joint, as shown. Repeat with the remaining short pieces of straw.

4 Take the thread back up through one of the half straws to the top of the structure. Tie another knot and then knot the thread ends together to form a hanging loop.

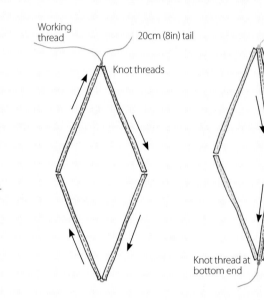

Working thread

20cm (8in) tail

Knot threads

Knot thread at bottom end

Take the thread back down one of the upper straws

Go through a short horizontal straw and then wrap thread around one of the centre joints

ARMILLARY SPHERE

YOU WILL NEED:

Large sheet of acetate
Thin patterned papers
Hole punch
Sticky notes (e.g., Post-It)
Brads or paper-fasteners
Patterned tissue paper
Polystyrene ball
Découpage medium
Two bamboo skewers
Large wooden bead
Small circular box (e.g., from cheese triangles)
Woodgrain paper
Small paper cone
PVA glue
Thin card
Dry rice or gravel

TECHNIQUE: Découpage

TIP / Don't be tempted to use card instead of acetate for the patterned strips, as it will crease at the intersections, giving the finished sphere corners instead of curves.

1 Cut three strips of acetate (see diagram). Glue patterned paper to both sides of the strips. Make five small holes in each one (as marked with red dots). Use sticky notes to mark the strips A, B and C.

2 Curve strip B round so the holes at the end overlap. Place the centre hole in strip A on top and push a brad through all three holes. Open out the ends to fix in place. Repeat, to join the ends of strip A to the centre hole in strip B. Use another brad to join the centre hole in strip C, to one of the remaining holes in strip A. Curve strip C around, overlapping the ends, and joining them to the last hole in strip A with a brad.

3 Tear patterned tissue into small pieces and use découpage medium to stick them to the polystyrene ball, overlapping the edges and smoothing out neatly with your fingers. Allow to dry. Push a bamboo skewer through the centre, so equal amounts protrude on each side. Slip the ends of the skewer through the holes in strips B and C, where they overlap.

4 Position the sphere so the skewer is at a diagonal angle. Punch an extra hole in the paper-covered strip directly below the polystyrene ball. Push a second skewer through the hole, through the centre of a wooden bead, and up into the base of the ball.

5 Fill the circular box with dry rice or gravel and tape the edges shut. Cover with woodgrain paper. Use a paper piercer to make a hole in the centre of the lid. Cover the paper cone with woodgrain paper and snip off a few millimetres at the pointed end to create a hole.

6 Push the end of the second bamboo skewer down through the hole in the cone and then through the lid of the round box. Cut off any excess skewer with scissors, before gluing the base of the cone to the box lid.

7 Copy the arrowhead and flight templates twice onto thin card and cut out. Glue the arrowheads back to back over the top end of the diagonal skewer, and the flights back to back over the bottom end.

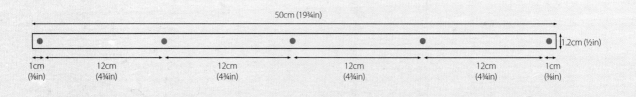

50cm (19¾in)

1.2cm (½in)

1cm (⅜in) 12cm (4¾in) 12cm (4¾in) 12cm (4¾in) 12cm (4¾in) 1cm (⅜in)

TECHNIQUES

Most of the projects in the book use basic skills and everyday tools and materials. This section gives advice and instructions on the more specialized tools and materials you might need, and also the specific methods used for some of the projects. The main technique categories are listed alphabetically: Collage, Découpage, Folding + Scoring, Jewellery, Papercutting, Papier Mâché, Sewing on Paper, Stamping + Embossing.

Collage

Collages can be abstract, figurative, typographic or pattern based. You can layer pieces on top of each other, overlap the edges, butt them up together for a patchwork kind of effect, or arrange them so they don't touch at all – it's up to you, and will probably depend entirely on the design you're working with. This can either be built freestyle, cutting and arranging the paper as you go along, or worked using a template. The latter is sometimes referred to as paper piecing, and is a little like making a paper jigsaw.

To add extra dimension or interest, you may want to use mixed media, incorporating other materials into your paper collage. Try using paint, tape, yarn, sequins, ribbon or small, recycled elements.

Tools

- **Paper** – you can use just about any kind of paper to make a collage, and it's generally fine, often hugely effective, to include a mixture of different types on a single piece. Combine plain sheets with patterns, new pieces with recycled finds, and mix different textures or thicknesses to add even more interest.
- **Adhesive** – the type of adhesive you use will depend on the type of paper you're using and the surface or base on which you're building the collage. Thicker paper, especially used on a solid or shiny surface (e.g., metal or plastic), will generally require a stronger adhesive than gluing medium-weight pieces to a paper or card base. Many collage artists fix pieces with gel medium, which you can find in art stores or the paint section of craft and hobby shops, but in most cases, PVA (white glue) or a glue stick will work just as well.
- **Substrates** – you can apply collage to a range of surfaces, including wood, metal, plastic and cardboard, although it's most often built on a simple paper base. This should ideally be a fairly thick or heavyweight paper to support the pieces on top – watercolour paper is ideal. This is particularly important if you're planning to work with different types or weights of paper, as they will create different types of strain on the base layer.

How to Construct a Collage

- Gather your paper pieces together and, if possible, arrange them on your background.
- Move things around and make any adjustments to ensure you're happy with the design and then, one at a time, glue the pieces into position.
- To make sure they're fully adhered, rub over the surface – paying particular attention to the edges – with the side of your hand, a brayer or an old rolling pin.

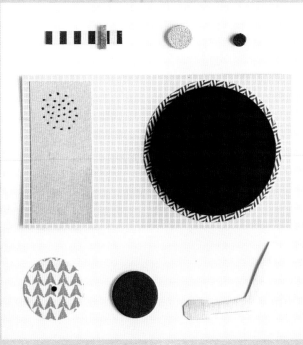

See Record Player Invitation

How to Work with Templates

- To use a template, or turn a drawing into a collage, start by tracing each of the pieces of the image onto translucent paper (this can be regular tracing paper or baking parchment/greaseproof paper from the kitchen).
- Transfer the pieces, one at a time, onto the back of your chosen papers. Select patterns and colours that will coordinate once you piece the image together; if you're uncertain about a particular detail, it's worth cutting that piece from a few different types of paper so you can try them out before committing to the finished design.
- Cut out each of the pieces and arrange them on your base or background. Once you're happy with how they look, glue each one firmly into place.

Découpage

Découpage is a technique that sounds much grander and more difficult than it is. Essentially, it involves gluing cut or torn pieces of paper onto the surface of an object. The finished effect can vary enormously depending on the type of paper you use and the item you're decorating.

You can apply découpage to many different surfaces (substrates), including wood, metal, cardboard, plastic and canvas. Any existing imperfections are likely to show up in the finished piece, so make any small repairs before you start (e.g., sanding wood splinters or snipping off loose canvas threads) and wipe the surface completely clean of any dust or grit. If the item you're decorating is very smooth or shiny, roughen it with a fine-grade sandpaper (wiping away the dust when you've finished) to help the glue adhere more easily.

Tools
- **Paper** – as a rule of thumb, soft, thin papers are best for découpage projects, particularly if you're decorating small items or something with lots of curves and details. As with papier mâché, the aim is to create as smooth and flat a finish as possible, and thinner papers make this much easier. You can buy patterned tissue that is specifically designed for découpage, or try lightweight gift wrap, old book pages, maps, pages from magazines or patterned origami papers. As most découpage adhesive is water based, don't use inkjet copies or anything else that isn't waterproof, as the colours will run and smudge.
- **Adhesives** – you can use PVA or white glue, but a découpage medium, such as Mod Podge, tends to create fewer bubbles and wrinkles in the paper. It dries to a tough, clear finish, so you can also use it to seal and protect the finished project, eliminating the need to buy a separate varnish. It's available in a range of finishes, including matte, satin and high gloss (the most traditional option for découpage).

> **TIP /** Tissue or other types of very thin paper may be semi-translucent, which means the base colour of your object will show through. If this is likely to cause a problem, brush or spray on a coat of white paint and allow it to dry before you start decorating.

How to Découpage
- Découpage is applied in a similar way to papier mâché. Ideally, tear the paper into strips or pieces, as this helps them stick together more easily and gives a smoother finish. If, however, you want to create a specific pattern – for instance, stripes or blocks of colour – you can cut the edges instead. Pay particular attention to them when you're gluing the pieces into place and make sure they're stuck down as securely as possible. The thinner your paper, the easier this will be.

- Once you've prepared the paper, spread a thin layer of adhesive over a small area of the object you want to decorate and press a piece of paper down on top. Use your fingers to smooth away any wrinkles or air bubbles, working from the centre out towards the edges. On large or flat pieces, you might find it's helpful to smooth the paper down with a brayer or an old rolling pin.
- Keep adding pieces of paper, overlapping the edges and applying adhesive to just a small area at a time. Keep going until you've covered the whole item, or as much of it as you want to decorate. While you need to apply multiple layers to papier mâché projects, a single one is enough for découpaged pieces.
- When the glue is dry, brush two to three layers of adhesive or varnish on top. Allow each one to dry before adding the next.

See Wooden Bead Necklace

> **TIP /** Some people find it easier to spread adhesive over the back of the paper, rather than applying it to the surface of the object – experiment and find out which method you prefer.

How to do Napkin Découpage

This is done with paper table napkins. They can either be used as described above or you can cut out specific details for a different kind of look.

- Select the details you want to use and trim closely around the outside edges. You only need to use the top, printed layer of the napkin, so once you've cut out the shape, carefully peel away any extra layers and discard. Position the printed pieces on your item to build up a design. You can use just one or two motifs, or layer lots of them to create a more detailed image.

- Once you're happy, lift the images off and brush a thin layer of adhesive onto the item. Place the napkin pieces very gently onto the adhesive, one at a time, and press into place. They're much more fragile than paper, so you'll need to handle them carefully to avoid tearing.

- When the glue is dry, brush on two to three additional coats of découpage medium or varnish to seal and protect.

See Flower Jars and Alphabet Blocks

Folding + Scoring

Folding a piece of paper or card may seem completely straightforward, but taking a little extra time to make the right sort of fold and ensuring it's crisp and neat, will give projects a sleeker, more professional finish.

Tools

1. Stylus – this is like a ballpoint pen, but with no ink. It's a good, general papercrafting tool, which is particularly useful for scoring smooth, straight lines. You can use the back (non-cutting) edge of a craft knife or small pair of scissors instead, but make sure to hold these at an angle while scoring, so the point doesn't nick or tear the paper.

2. Bone folder – this is a hard, plastic tool with a flat edge, used to press and flatten creases or folds. They sometimes have a sharp tip that can also be used for scoring. At a pinch, you could use a clean wooden lollipop stick instead.

3. Ruler – used to measure and score perfectly straight lines. Choose a metal one and you can also use it with a craft knife for cutting straight edges. Look out for non-slip versions, which have a flat rubber strip along the back, to reduce the chances of the ruler moving as you cut and score.

4. Self-healing cutting mat – you can find these in a wide range of sizes and use them as a working surface for many paper-based projects. They're made from a plastic that 'heals' or repairs itself after you cut into it. As well as giving the mat a longer working life, this also prolongs the life of your blades, blunting them far less quickly than other cutting surfaces, such as glass mats. A mat isn't essential for scoring – if you don't have one, work on a protected surface so you don't damage or mark the area beneath your work.

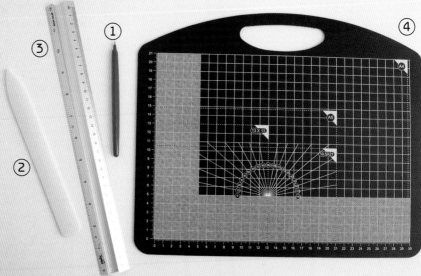

How to Score Paper or Card

- Scoring involves making an indentation in your paper or card before you fold it along the same line. It creates much crisper, more accurate folds, and avoids unsightly wrinkles and cracks in glossy or coated paper.

- To score a straight line (as when folding a piece of card in half) use a ruler to find the centre of the card and mark this with a tiny pencil dot at the top and bottom edges.

- Line the ruler up against the dots, but instead of using a pencil, 'draw' the line with a stylus or scoring tool. Pull it slowly towards you, along the edge of the ruler, applying even pressure.

- When you've finished, neatly fold the card along the scored line. To make the fold even sharper, press firmly along it from top to bottom using the flat edge of a bone folder.

TIP/ The thinner the paper, the less pressure you need to apply when scoring, and vice versa. You're aiming to make an indentation, not to tear or drag the paper as you score.

How to Make Valley and Mountain Folds

- Paper can be folded upwards (a mountain fold), or downwards (a valley fold). The direction is related to the front (or patterned) side of the paper. A standard greetings card, for instance, uses a mountain fold. The pattern is on the outside, with the folded edge at the top, forming a mountain shape.

- A valley fold is the opposite – the pattern appears on the inside, with the fold at the bottom, forming a V shape.

- Accordion folding alternates between the two – forwards/backwards/forwards/backwards, or valley/mountain/valley/mountain – to form an accordion or simple fan shape.

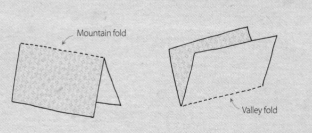

Mountain fold

Valley fold

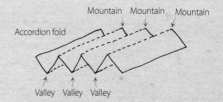

Accordion fold

Mountain Mountain Mountain

Valley Valley Valley

Jewellery

There are a number of jewellery projects in the book, which are very satisfying to make, and perfect to give as gifts.

Wire

Jewellery wire comes in different numbered gauges. The lower the number, the finer (thinner) the wire is. If you're buying it in a shop, you can generally tell by flexing the wire between your fingers whether it's too stiff or too bendy, too thick or too thin, for your project. Obviously that's not possible when shopping online, but all of the wire jewellery projects in this book include a note of the gauge used as a handy guide.

Tools

The only tool you need for the jewellery projects in this book is a small pair of general purpose pliers. You could also invest in a couple of pairs specifically for jewellery making, as follows.

- **Chain-nosed pliers** – these have a fine, tapered point that makes them perfect for small projects, like necklaces and pendants. The inside edges or jaws are flat, so they can easily grip and twist wire.

- **Cutter pliers** – also known as wire cutters, these are useful for trimming wire and also snipping through the links in a chain to adjust the length.

Findings

Findings are the materials used to make or link pieces of jewellery together. You can buy them inexpensively via online jewellery shops or in craft and hobby stores. Alternatively, raid your jewellery box for pieces you no longer wear and re-purpose the components. Things like beads, chains and clasps can easily be separated and re-used.

1. Chain – this comes in a wide range of different weights, sizes and finishes. You can either buy short lengths that already have clasps at the end, or longer pieces that can be cut to size, ready for you to add your own clasp or closure.

2. Clasps – these are used to hold the ends of a necklace or bracelet together. The most common types are spring-rings and lobster claws, both of which can be fixed in place with a simple jump ring (see below).

3. Leather thong or cord – this is sold on reels or by the metre/yard. It can be used as an alternative to a chain in some projects, with the ends tied together in place of using clasps. Try faux leather or cotton thong if you'd prefer not to use the real thing.

4. Pendant blanks – sometimes called pendant trays, these are tiny frames generally made from wood, metal or resin. Available in a wide range of shapes and sizes, they have a gap of some kind in the centre, ready to add your own decoration or design.

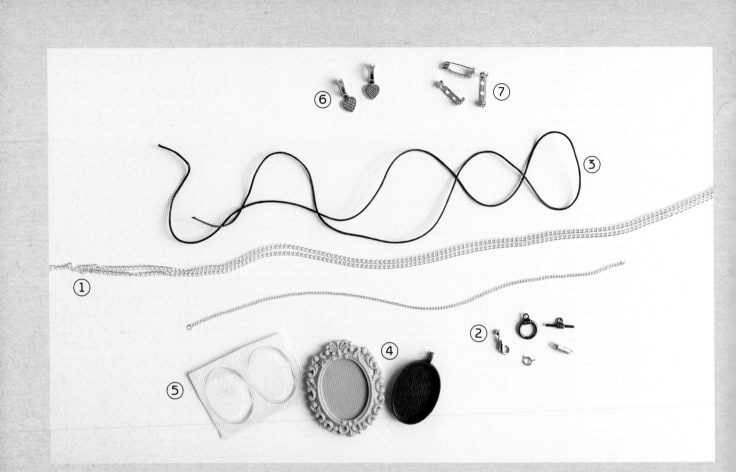

5. Cabochons – these are clear glass or plastic domes that fit inside the frame part of a pendant blank. You can use them as an optional way of sealing your chosen design in place.

6. Bails – these are tiny metal components, used to link a pendant to a chain. If your pendant blank doesn't have a ring or loop at the top, you'll need to glue a bail to the back instead. The simplest kind is shaped like the letter P, with a flat base and a loop above.

7. Brooch backs – these work a little like safety pins. The sharp, pin-like side opens out from a secure clip, and the opposite side is flat so it can be glued (or stitched) to the back of your project.

8. Jump rings – possibly the most useful and versatile of jewellery findings, these small metal rings, have a gap or split that allows them to be temporarily opened and closed. Generally used as links to connect components or findings, they come in a range of metallic finishes so you can match them to your project. Jump rings should always be opened out sideways. Pulling them apart in any other way can weaken or distort the shape of the ring, putting the pieces of your finished jewellery piece at risk of falling apart. To open the ring sideways, grip it between your thumb and index finger to one side of the split, and hold the other side with a pair of pliers. Move the pliers towards you and your other hand away from you, so the ring opens out just a few millimetres. Once you've linked or attached it to the relevant component, reverse the process to close the gap again.

Papercutting

Papercutting can be used to create beautiful, intricate works of art, slightly simpler silhouette shapes or useful, detailed stencils. It can appear quite overwhelming at first, but with a steady hand, a little patience and the most basic of tools, anyone can achieve impressive results.

Tools

- **Craft knife** – these are widely available and fairly inexpensive. It can take a while to get used to the feel of cutting with a knife if you're used to scissors, but practise making freehand cuts on some scrap paper, and you'll quickly get the hang of it. Craft knives are available with metal or rubber handles. Papercutting can be quite time consuming, so rubber is often the more comfortable option. Use a self-healing cutting mat with craft knives (see Folding + Scoring).

- **Spare blades** – blades are usually generic and will fit most knives. Keep a small stock of them, so you can change the blade regularly. It sounds strange, but the safest knife is a sharp knife. You need to apply less pressure to cut with a fresh, sharp blade, which reduces the likelihood of the knife slipping and cutting you.

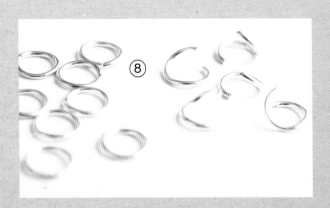

- **Paper** – medium-weight paper is the best option if you're new to papercutting. It's easy to slice through, but not so fragile that it tears easily. Pick papers with a smooth, flat surface as these make for crisp, clean paper cuts. Handmade paper or anything very soft tends to have loose fibres, which can make the cut edges look blurred. The knife is also more likely to drag the paper as you cut. It's a good idea to work with lighter shades, to more easily see the design outline and where you're cutting. If you want your finished project to be a darker colour, look out for coated papers, which have colour on one side and white on the reverse. You can then cut from the back, before flipping the design over to display the colourful side.

How to Papercut

- Draw or trace a design onto the back of your paper in pencil. Bear in mind the image will be reversed when you turn it over, so if it includes details like numbers and letters, or anything that needs to face a specific way, flip the design before you start.

- Place the paper on your cutting mat and, holding the knife as you would a pen, begin cutting along the lines of the design. Apply a light, even pressure and pull the knife towards you – you'll quickly get the hang of how hard you need to press to cut through the paper. Hold the paper steady with your other hand as you cut, and rotate it as often as you need. Bear in mind you're usually cutting out the pieces you need to discard and the finished design is made up of the paper left behind.

- Be patient and take your time. Rushing leads to mistakes and they can be hard to correct. Cut over a few days or sessions if needs be, and aim for a state of relaxed concentration.

Papier Mâché

Papier mâché can be used to add strength, texture and uniformity to a paper or cardboard model, or to construct a stand-alone item worked around a simple mould, such as a bowl or balloon. When built up in layers, it can also add dimension to a flat cardboard shape. It is a little time-consuming, but straightforward, versatile and very inexpensive.

Tools

- **Paper** – use papers that are thin and fairly soft. Old newspapers or pages from a telephone directory are perfect. Tissue paper creates a slightly finer kind of papier mâché, and is especially good for small projects. If you want your finished object to be a solid colour and you can find the right shade of tissue, it can also save you having to paint it.

- **Paste** – traditional papier mâché paste recipes usually involve flour and water, but it's more convenient and less messy to use store-bought wallpaper paste. The dry powder can be stored in an airtight container, and the mixed paste also keeps well. To mix, follow the instructions on the packaging, but use a little less water than advised to make a thicker, stickier paste. The end result should soak right into your paper and dry out to give a tough finish.

TIP/ As well as cutting pieces away from the background, you can also make small cuts or nicks in the surface with your knife, to add interesting texture and detail to large or flat areas of paper.

See Papercut Map

How to Use a Mould

- Anything that can easily be removed from the finished object can be used as a mould, for instance, a bowl, a straight-sided drinking glass or a small box.

- Cover the object with cling film (plastic wrap) to stop the papier mâché sticking to it. Allow plenty of excess around the top edge to lift the mould out after the paste has set.

- Balloons are traditionally used to mould piñatas. By leaving a small hole around the knot, you can pierce the balloon once the papier mâché has set and pull out the deflated balloon. The hole can then be covered with a few extra strips of pasted paper.

How to Build Layers

- To cover a mould or cardboard model with papier mâché, start by tearing the paper into strips. The size will depend on the shape and size of your project – the smaller or more intricate the mould or model, the smaller the strips should be. It's also important to tear them (don't use scissors) as this creates rough, 'feathered' edges that are easier to stick down and give a smoother, more even surface.

- Take a paper strip, and using your fingers or a small brush, cover both sides in a layer of paste. Press down onto the mould or model and smooth it out to remove lumps or air bubbles. Add more strips in the same way, overlapping the edges and placing them at different angles, until the whole piece is covered. The picture shows a bowl in progress.

- Add a second layer of paper strips on top of the first. It's helpful to use two different paper types or colours so you can see when you've completed each of the layers, e.g., regular newspaper for the first layer and yellow phone book pages for the second.

- Set the papier mâché aside to dry (see Drying). Add more layers on top, two at a time, until the piece is as tough as you'd like. For covered models, three to four layers should be fine; for moulded pieces, you'll probably need to add at least a couple more.

Drying

Papier mâché will dry most quickly outside on breezy summer days – the combination of warmth and plenty of moving air is perfect. If that's not possible, try an airing cupboard, sunny windowsill or shelf near a radiator. Place it on a surface it won't stick to, for instance a silicone baking sheet or piece of waxed paper.

Adding Colour

When the papier mâché is completely dry, you can paint it to add colour and patterns. Brush on a layer of white acrylic paint as a base coat, adding your chosen colour on top. Seal the finished design with one to two coats of clear varnish (matt or gloss).

TIP / Papier mâché must be completely dry, or paint will bubble, flake and fall off. Allow the pasted strips to dry overnight, or longer in cold weather.

Sewing on Paper

Stitching on paper is different, but not really any harder, than stitching on fabric.

Tools

- **Needles** – paper blunts needles far more quickly than fabric, so it's a good idea to set aside dedicated needles for this kind of stitching. Store them in a separate, labelled container or, for sewing machine needles, add a dot of nail polish to the shank so you can quickly identify that it's a paper needle.

- **Thread** – you can use normal, all-purpose sewing thread for fine stitching, both by hand and machine. Thicker threads are slightly trickier, but as long as you don't rush or pull them through the paper too quickly, they will work and can create interesting,

TIP / Papier mâché is pretty messy, so work over a wipe-clean surface, or cover the area with an old sheet. If you have sensitive skin, wear surgical gloves to protect your hands.

See Papier Mâché Dots Bowl

textured effects. Try using embroidery thread (all six strands for a chunky effect, or less if you prefer), fine yarn or baker's twine.

How to Stitch on Paper

- If your project needs to lie flat, avoid knotting threads when starting and finishing. They will either be visible or create lumps in the paper. The simplest alternative is to use sticky tape. Pull the threads taut against the back of your work, tape down neatly and then trim away any excess.
- You might find it easier when hand sewing to make the holes first. This can be especially helpful when sewing through several layers of paper at a time. Outline your design on the paper and then use a needle or piercing tool to stab small holes at regular intervals. Work with the paper on top of an old mouse mat or sheet of craft foam for best results.

TIP / A paper piercer is a useful general tool, but you can create a makeshift version by pushing the eye end of a needle into a cork. Hold the cork and use the pointed end of the needle to make the holes.

How to Machine Sew on Paper

- A basic sewing machine will do to stitch on paper.
- Stitch a little more slowly than you would on fabric, because mistakes are more visible and much harder to undo on paper.
- Keep your bobbin loaded, so you don't have to switch threads part-way through a project. Try to sew on the front (right side) of the paper as the holes look less neat from the back.
- Ideally, set the stitch length fairly long to reduce the risk of tearing. The one exception to this is using your machine to deliberately create perforations. In that case, use a shorter stitch length with no threads, for a line of holes that is perfect for tear-off strips on calendars or invitations. Paper can create a slightly dusty residue, so it's a good idea to clean your machine after use.

TIP / Experiment and practise on scrap paper to get used to stitching before you start your project.

How to Work Running Stitch

- Bring your needle up through the paper and then back down a stitch length away (you can make stitches long or short, as preferred).
- Bring it back up at roughly the same distance apart and then make a second stitch in the same way. Continue, building up an even row of stitches with evenly sized gaps between.

How to Work Backstitch

- Make a single straight stitch and then bring your needle back up through the paper a stitch length away (A, B).
- Take the thread back down through the end of the first stitch and back up a stitch length away from the end of the second stitch. Take it back down through the end of the second stitch (C, D).
- Keep going to build up a smooth, solid line of stitches.

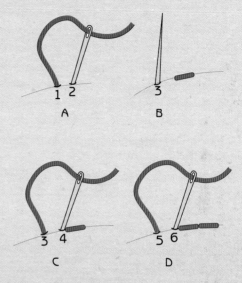

How to Work Cross Stitch

- Working on a grid or large-scale graph paper, bring your needle up through the corner of one square and then back down in the opposite corner to make a diagonal stitch (A).
- Bring the needle up through one of the remaining corners, and then back down in the opposite one to finish the X (B).
- Work another stitch in the same way, starting in the bottom-left corner of the first X. Keep going, adding more cross stitches to build up your pattern or design (C).

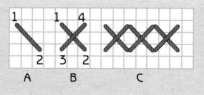

TIP / On small-scale graph paper, stitch across two or three squares at a time, so your stitches are still even, but not too tiny. To work cross stitch on plain paper, stitch each cross freehand, leaving gaps in between for an irregular but pretty effect.

Stamping and Embossing

When stamping and embossing remember that different types of ink create different impressions, depending on the type of paper you use. Generally, the smoother and flatter the surface, the sharper the stamped image will be. Matt-effect papers can soak up ink, causing it to bleed at the edges. Handmade or textured papers are also likely to distort the finished impression, particularly if it's an intricate design. Glossy papers are more able to hold detailed designs, but your stamp may slip around on the shiny surface, causing a different kind of distortion. Experiment with different inks and stamp designs, practising on scrap paper to see what works, before embarking on a new project.

Types of Stamp

1. Rubber – rubber stamps are usually mounted onto a small block of wood, which makes them easy to handle. They're tough, long lasting and generally give a sharp, clear impression. You can use them with all kinds of ink, and they also work well into paper clay. They tend to be more expensive than other types of stamp and are bulkier to store. It's also harder to see exactly where you're stamping, as both the rubber and the wooden block are opaque. Some companies now sell un-mounted rubber stamps with a peel-off adhesive backing. This allows you to fix them to a clear acrylic stamp block, combining the advantages of rubber with the convenience of acrylic stamps.

2. Acrylic – clear acrylic stamps, also known as polymer or photo-polymer stamps, are used along with a clear stamping block. These come in various sizes and, as the stamps easily peel off after use, a single block can be used no matter how many stamps you have.

The stamps are generally sold in sets, making them very economical, and take up little storage space. Acrylic stamp designs are often more contemporary or trend-led than those found on rubber stamps and their transparency means you can see exactly where you're making each stamped impression. Despite their convenience, the detail on acrylic stamps tends to be a little less sharp than on rubber, and they're also more fragile. Depending on the type of ink you use, the acrylic can become stained and some stamps may also degenerate over time.

3. Foam – foam stamps are less common than rubber or acrylic. They create chunkier images and are best used with acrylic paints, rather than ink, which can add interesting texture and scale. Foam stamps are also effective on other surfaces, such as fabric, furniture and walls. The range of designs tends to be more limited, and it can be hard to create a clean, even impression with foam.

4. Erasers – simple erasers can also be used as stamps. Look out for the novelty, shaped kind (often found in kitschy or teen stationery ranges). They create very basic, solid shapes, rather than detailed impressions, but are inexpensive and good for creating patterns or layers.

Types of Ink

- **Dye-based ink** – these inks are inexpensive and dry almost instantly on porous surfaces. Colours are slightly transparent, which is good for soft pastels and strong, bright shades. The ink is less effective on glossy papers, and may struggle to dry on these. It can gather in bubbles or pools on acrylic stamps, creating impressions that are much duller and less clear than those made with a rubber stamp. The ink is not waterproof and colours are prone to fading over time.

TIP / To try stamping with little or no expense, grab a pencil with an (unused) eraser at the end, and use the eraser to stamp spots over a piece of paper. Use acrylic paint or a basic inkpad and experiment to create both random and more even polka dot patterns.

- **Pigment ink** – this creates clean, sharp images and works well with most kinds of stamps. It's thicker and denser than dye-based ink and takes longer to dry, but is the best coloured ink to use with embossing powders. It's fade resistant and works on both porous and glossy surfaces, although may require heat setting to dry on the latter.
- **Solvent-based ink** – this is waterproof and perfect for using with paint or marker pens. It makes clear, sharp impressions, even with very detailed stamps, and dries almost instantly on porous surfaces. The ink takes just a little longer to set on glossy or shiny paper, but once dry, is permanent and fade resistant.
- **Watermark ink** – this is clear and slightly sticky. It creates a subtle, tone-on-tone effect (like a watermark) on coloured paper and dries fairly slowly. It's particularly effective for embossing, as the clear base allows you to use any colour powder on top.

Storage

Always store inkpads flat. With dye-based ink in particular, keeping them tipped at an angle can lead to uneven coverage on your stamps. As they age, it's useful to store pads upside down (but still flat), so the remaining ink stays nearer the surface. Pigment inks are often sold with a thin plastic cover that fits over the top of the pad. This keeps air out, which in turns helps the ink to stay fresh and moist, so don't throw it away.

How to Stamp

- Place paper on a smooth, flat surface, such as a table or counter.
- Hold the stamp in one hand, face up. Hold the inkpad in your other hand. Tap the inkpad gently but firmly all over the surface of the stamp until evenly covered with ink.
- Set the inkpad aside, turn the stamp over and press it down firmly onto the paper. Apply gentle pressure for a few seconds, without moving your hands or taking them off the stamp.
- Lift the stamp straight up off the paper to reveal the image. If the stamp sticks, hold the paper with one hand and lift the stamp up with the other.

Troubleshooting

- If parts of the design are missing, you might not have inked the stamp evenly, or pressed it down firmly enough. It's also possible the surface under the paper might be uneven (more likely to be a problem if you're using an acrylic stamp). Try placing a magazine or an old mouse mat under the paper so it has a little more 'give' as you stamp.
- If your stamped image looks messy or has extra ink marks around the outside, you may have pressed down too hard when inking the stamp. Squashing the pad into the design rather than tapping it over the surface can transfer too much ink and distort the finished impression.

Heat Embossing

Heat embossing a stamped image gives it a glossy, slightly raised finish. The end result looks smart and professional, but is easier to achieve than you might think. Embossing powders come in a wide range of colours and finishes, including metallic and glitter effects. Most solid colours will cover up the ink used to stamp the image, but it may still show around the edges. This can create interesting effects, but if you want a clean, single-colour finish, you either need to match the ink and powder colours, or ensure one of them is colourless, i.e., use a clear watermark inkpad with coloured embossing powder or a clear embossing powder with coloured ink.

TIP / A heating tool, also known as a heat gun, emits a very high-temperature, dry heat. It's a small investment, but worthwhile if you want to experiment with heat embossing.

How to Emboss

- Stamp your image (as described in How to Stamp), using a pigment or watermark ink. Sprinkle embossing powder over the top before the ink dries. Shake the excess back into the pot, so the powder just adheres to the stamped design.
- To activate the powder, hold a heating tool 10–15cm (4–6in) away from the paper and watch as the powder melts and becomes glossy. You may need to move the heating tool around to melt the whole design, especially if it's quite large.
- Stop as soon as all of the powder has melted, or the embossing will become dull and flat.

Image before heating

Image after heating

How to Clean Up

- Stamps used with water-based inks can easily be cleaned with a damp paper towel or alcohol-free baby wipe.
- If the back of an acrylic stamp is sticky, add a little dish soap to the water to remove any dirt it may have attracted. An old toothbrush can also be useful for cleaning sticky pigment inks out of the nooks and crannies in more intricate stamps.
- Solvent-based inks won't wash off with water, but you can buy special solvent cleaners. These are fine to use on rubber stamps, but can be quite damaging to acrylic and so should be used sparingly.

TEMPLATES

The templates here have been reduced to fit the book, either to half size or quarter size, so follow the photocopying instructions with each template to increase them to full size. Alternatively, you can download a printable PDF of the templates from the following website: www.stitchcraftcreate.co.uk/patterns

Mobile Phone Case

Shown half size, so enlarge by 200% on a photocopier

Head and body
Cut 1 from flesh-toned card

Shirt
Cut 1 from patterned paper

Magnetic Paper Quilt

Shown half size, so enlarge by 200% on a photocopier

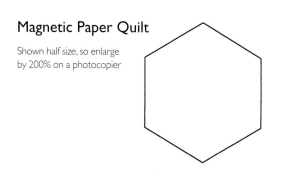

Paper Bow Garland

Shown half size, so enlarge by 200% on a photocopier

Centre strip

Collar
Cut 1 from patterned paper

Sweater
Cut 1 from patterned paper

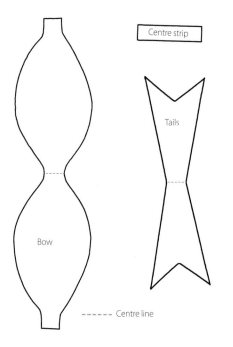

Tails

Bow

------ Centre line

Chevron Garland

Shown half size, so enlarge by 200% on a photocopier

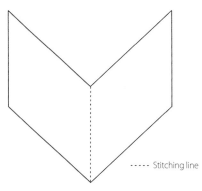

----- Stitching line

With-or-Without-a-Biscuit Coasters

Shown quarter size, so enlarge by 400% on a photocopier

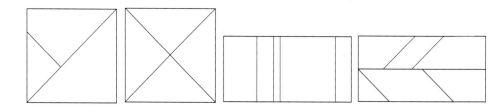

Paper Bead Pendants

Shown half size, so enlarge by 200%
on a photocopier

Spread glue over
shaded area

Tear-Out Matchbooks

Shown half size, so enlarge by 200%
on a photocopier

Matchbook Cover

A

Score along
dotted lines

B

Score along
dotted lines

C

Matchbook pages

- - - - - - - - - Perforation line

(do not write or print below this line)

Inside Out Envelopes

Shown quarter size, so enlarge by 400%
on a photocopier

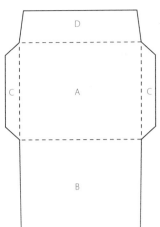

D

C   A   C

B

Stitched Love Photograph

Shown half size, so enlarge by 200%
on a photocopier

Camera Storage Box

Shown half size, so enlarge by 200%
on a photocopier

Lens

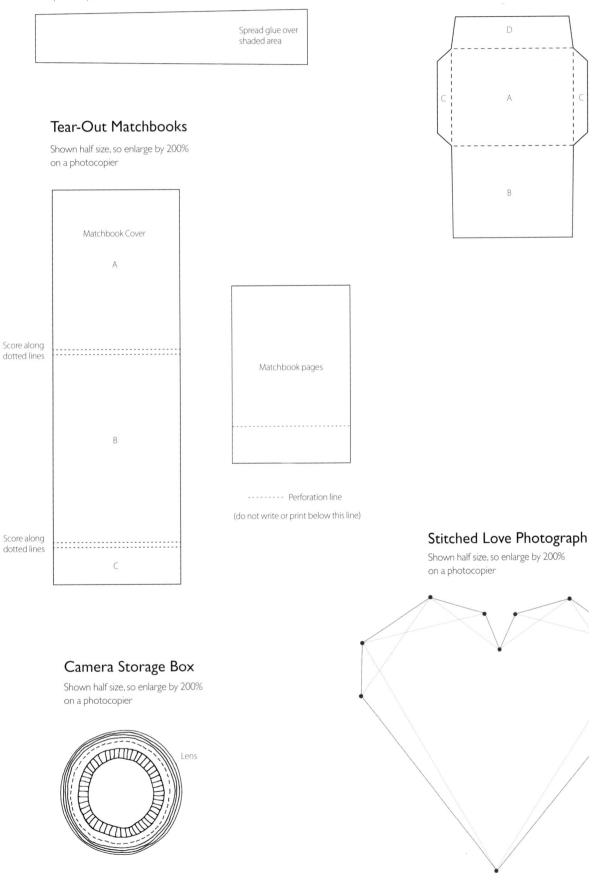

The Owl and the Pussycat

Shown half size, so enlarge by 200% on a photocopier

Boat
Cut 2 from pea green card

Joining strip
Cut 1 from pea green card

- - - - - Score and fold

.... Cut slits

Record Player Invitation

Shown half size, so enlarge by 200% on a photocopier

Deck base
Cut 1 from grid pattern (or similar)

Speaker panel

Cut 1 from plain card and draw on speaker dots with black marker pen

Record

Turntable

Record centre

Cut 4 or 5 from thin black card and glue together in a stack to create a chunky disc

Cut 1 from dark grey card

Cut 1 from patterned paper and draw a dot in the middle with a marker pen

Record arm support

Cut 1 from thick card

Arm/Stylus

Cut 3 from silver paper and glue together in a stack

Volume slider

Cut 1 from striped paper

Slider button

Cut 1 from woodgrain or metallic paper

Large button

Cut 1 from thick card and 1 from silver paper and glue paper on top of card

Small button

Cut 3 from card, two from red paper and 1 from silver paper and glue paper on top of card

Cut-Out Tangrams

Shown half size, so enlarge by 200% on a photocopier

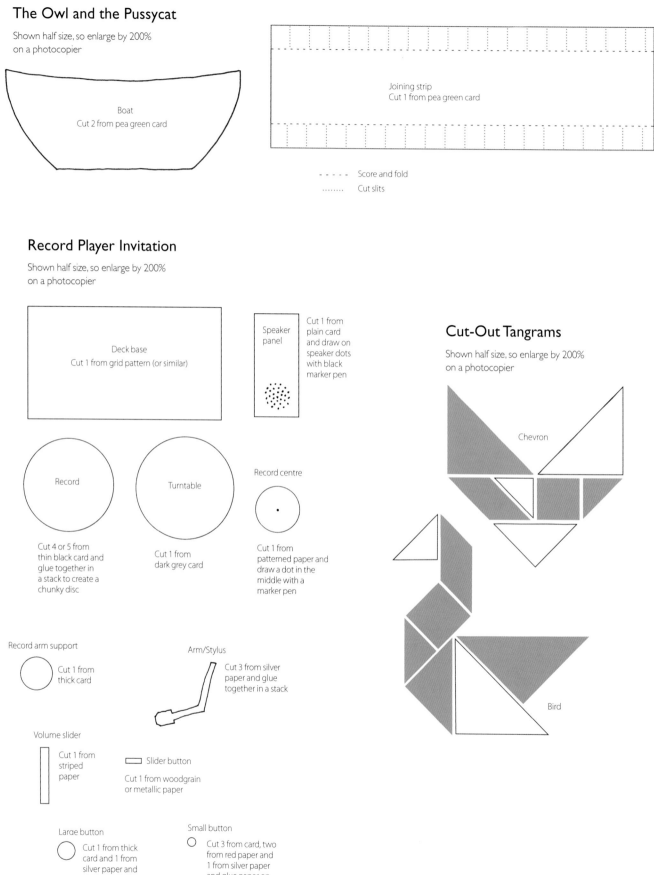

Chevron

Bird

Envelope Organizer

Label and label holder shown half size, so enlarge by 200% on a photocopier

Measurement template not to scale – follow the measurements given

Label holder

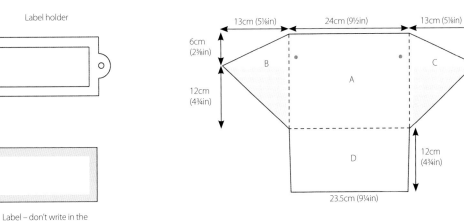

Label – don't write in the shaded sections

Apply glue to back of shaded areas

•   Add paper fasteners here

- - - - Score and fold along dotted lines

Paperville

Shown half size, so enlarge by 200% on a photocopier

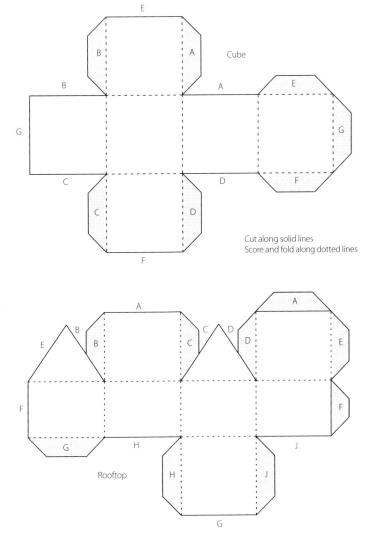

Cut along solid lines
Score and fold along dotted lines

Chalkboard Gift Tag

Shown half size, so enlarge by 200% on a photocopier

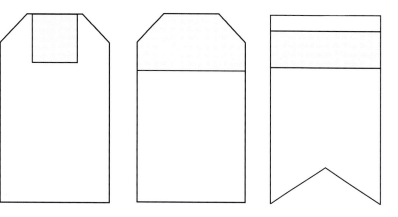

Cut shaded areas from patterned paper

Succulent Planters

Shown half size, so enlarge by 200% on a photocopier

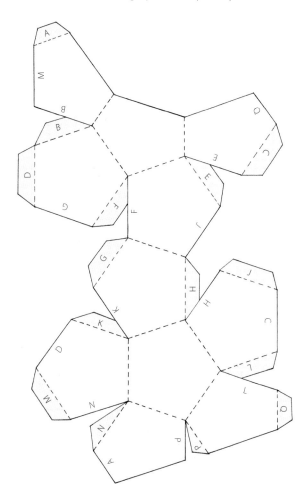

Flying Birds

Shown half size, so enlarge by 200% on a photocopier

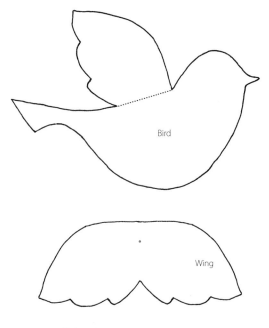

Bird

Wing

······ Fold along dotted line

• Add thread here

Transparent Favour Envelopes

Shown half size, so enlarge by 200% on a photocopier

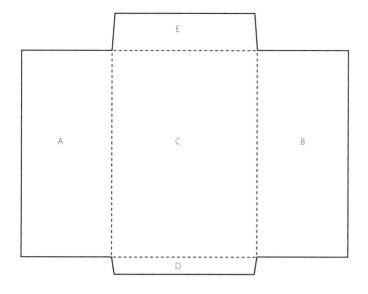

Papier Mâché Frida

Shown quarter size, so enlarge by 400% on a photocopier

Polaroid Charms

Shown half size, so enlarge by 200% on a photocopier

Mini Suitcase Storage

Shown half size, so enlarge by 200% on a photocopier

Handle
Cut 2 from card

Score and fold along the dotted lines

Half-Cut Cards

Shown half size, so enlarge by 200% on a photocopier

Wild Things Mask

Shown quarter size, so enlarge by 400% on a photocopier

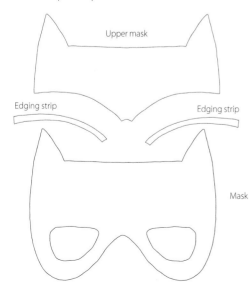

Upper mask

Edging strip   Edging strip

Mask

Make-an-Impression Wall Hanging

Shown half size, so enlarge by 200% on a photocopier

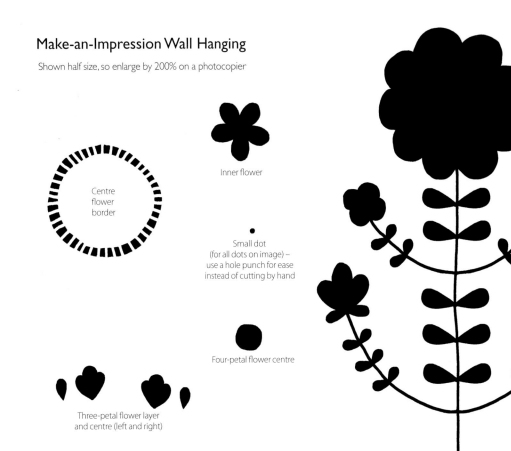

Centre
flower
border

Inner flower

Small dot
(for all dots on image) –
use a hole punch for ease
instead of cutting by hand

Four-petal flower centre

Three-petal flower layer
and centre (left and right)

You're-a-Star Shaker Card

Shown half size, so enlarge by 200% on
a photocopier

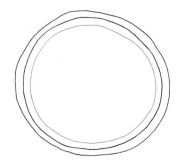

Folded Card Holder

Shown half size, so enlarge by
200% on a photocopier

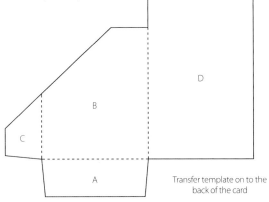

D

B

C

A

Transfer template on to the
back of the card

DIY Stamps

Shown half size, so enlarge by 200% on a photocopier

Paper-Pieced Portrait

Shown quarter size, so enlarge by 400% on a photocopier

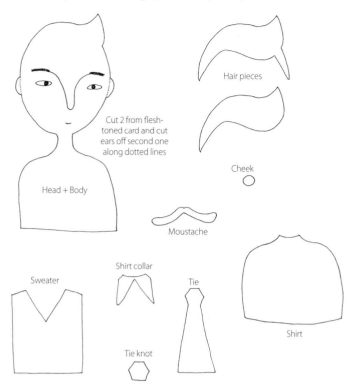

Hair pieces

Cut 2 from flesh-toned card and cut ears off second one along dotted lines

Head + Body

Cheek

Moustache

Sweater

Shirt collar

Tie

Shirt

Tie knot

Geometric Jewellery

Shown half size, so enlarge by 200% on a photocopier

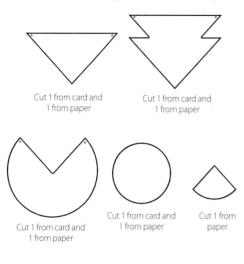

Cut 1 from card and 1 from paper

Cut 1 from card and 1 from paper

Cut 1 from card and 1 from paper

Cut 1 from card and 1 from paper

Cut 1 from paper

Faux Letterpress Poster

Shown half size, so enlarge by 200% on a photocopier

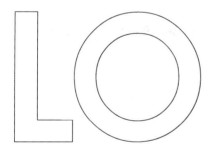

Go-for-Gold Notebooks

Shown half size, so enlarge by 200% on a photocopier

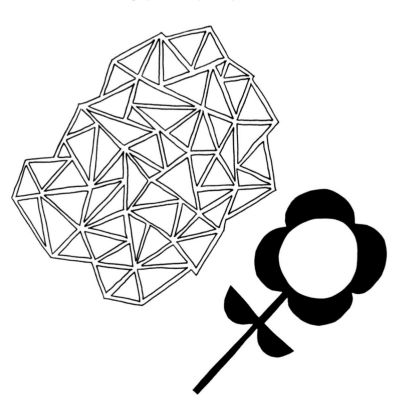

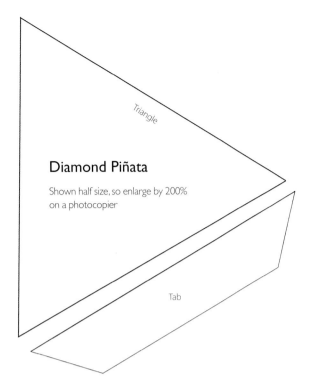

Diamond Piñata

Shown half size, so enlarge by 200% on a photocopier

Triangle

Tab

Fancy Sticking Plasters

Shown half size, so enlarge by 200% on a photocopier

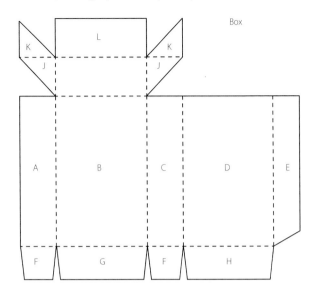

Box

Blossoms + Branch

Shown half size, so enlarge by 200% on a photocopier

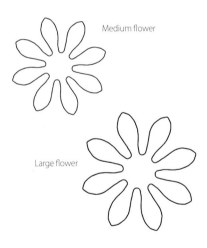

Medium flower

Large flower

Geometric Papercuts

Shown half size, so enlarge by 200% on a photocopier

Screen-Printed Mats

Shown quarter size, so enlarge by 400% on a photocopier

Armillary Sphere

Shown half size, so enlarge by 200% on a photocopier

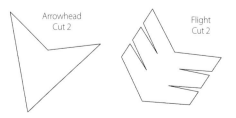

Arrowhead
Cut 2

Flight
Cut 2

CUT-OUT SHEETS

The projects on the following pages are ready to cut out and make straight away. Some of them, for instance the Easy-Fold Box, are double-sided, using the front and the back of the page. Those that are single-sided all have a full sheet of patterned paper on the reverse. You can either choose to cut out the project pieces and use the patterned side as leftover scraps, **or** photocopy the sheet and use both sides in full.

Fold + Stitch DIY Books

Hipster Merit Badges

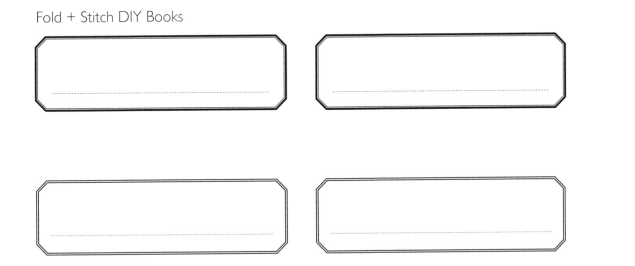

| Animal Lover | Bookworm | Nature lover | Writer | Photographer |

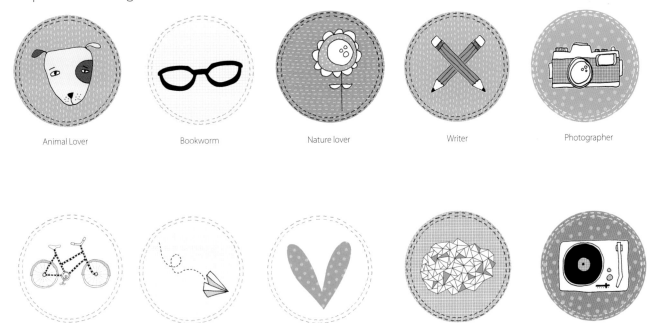

| Cyclist | Papercrafter | Friend | Scientist | Musician |

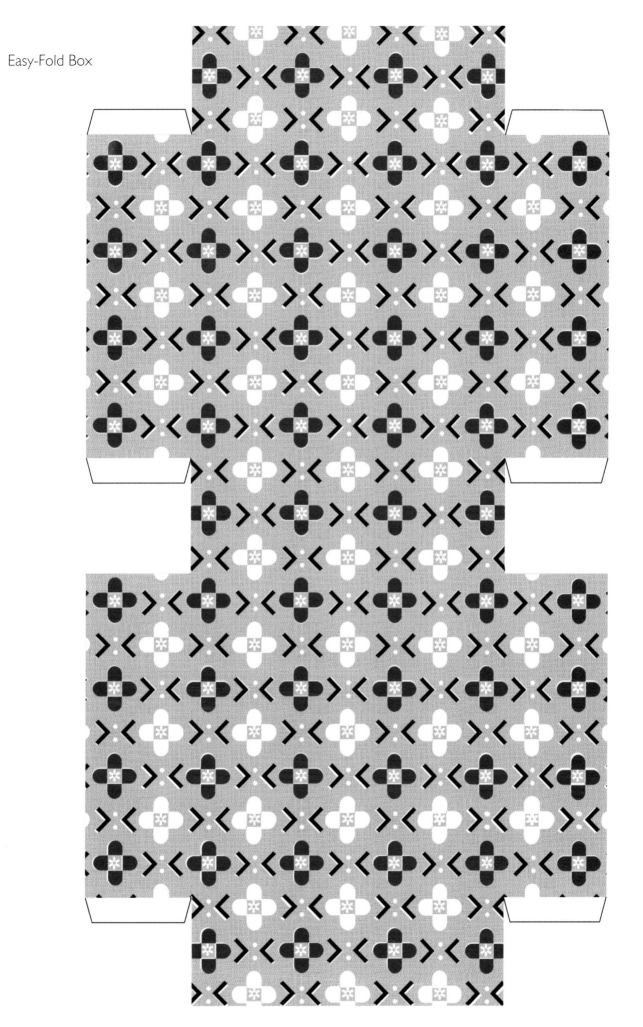

Easy-Fold Box

Magnetic Memo Clips

Graph Paper Cross Stitch

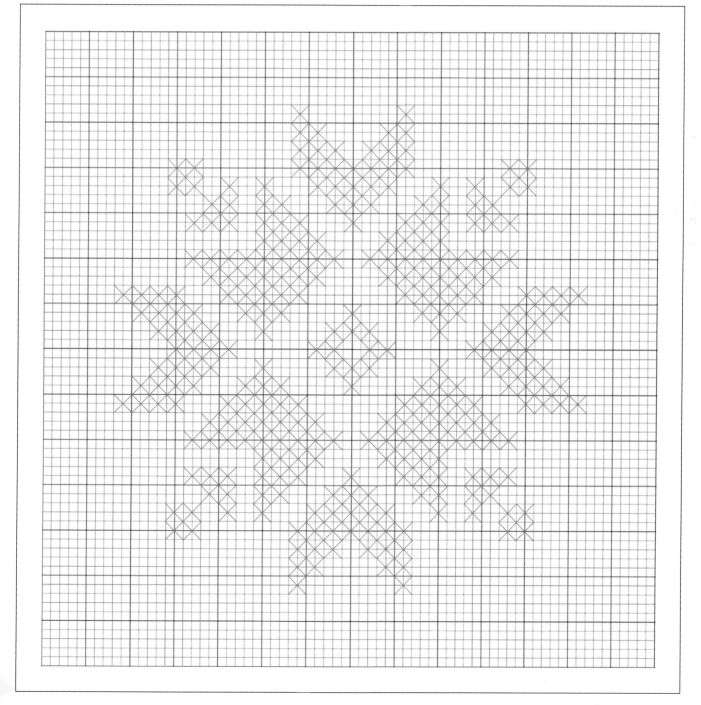

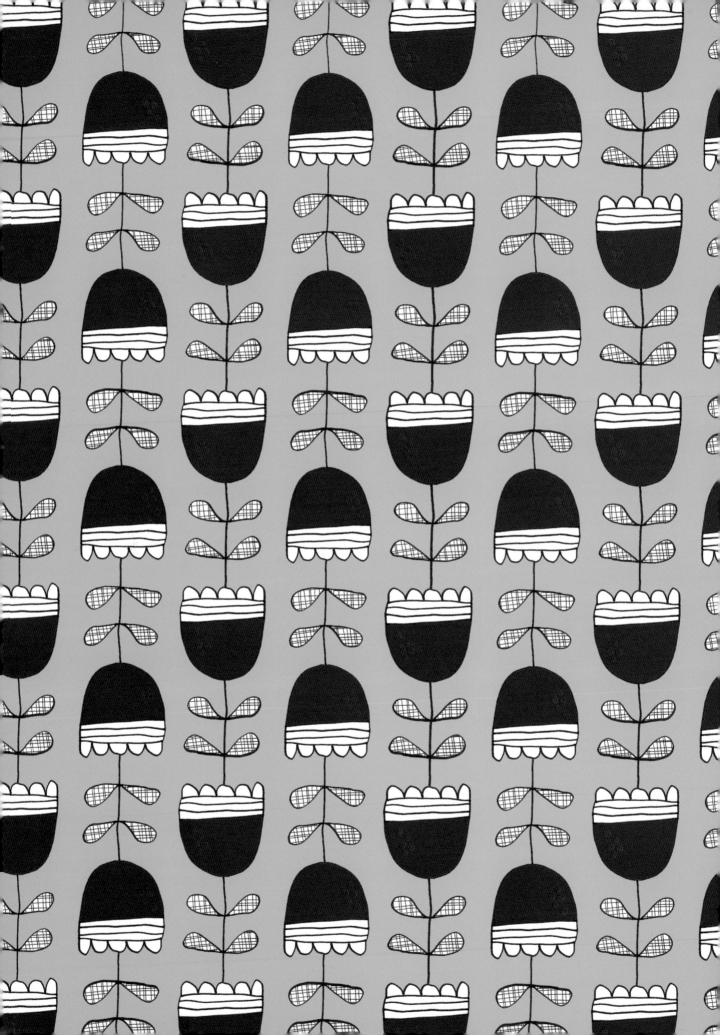

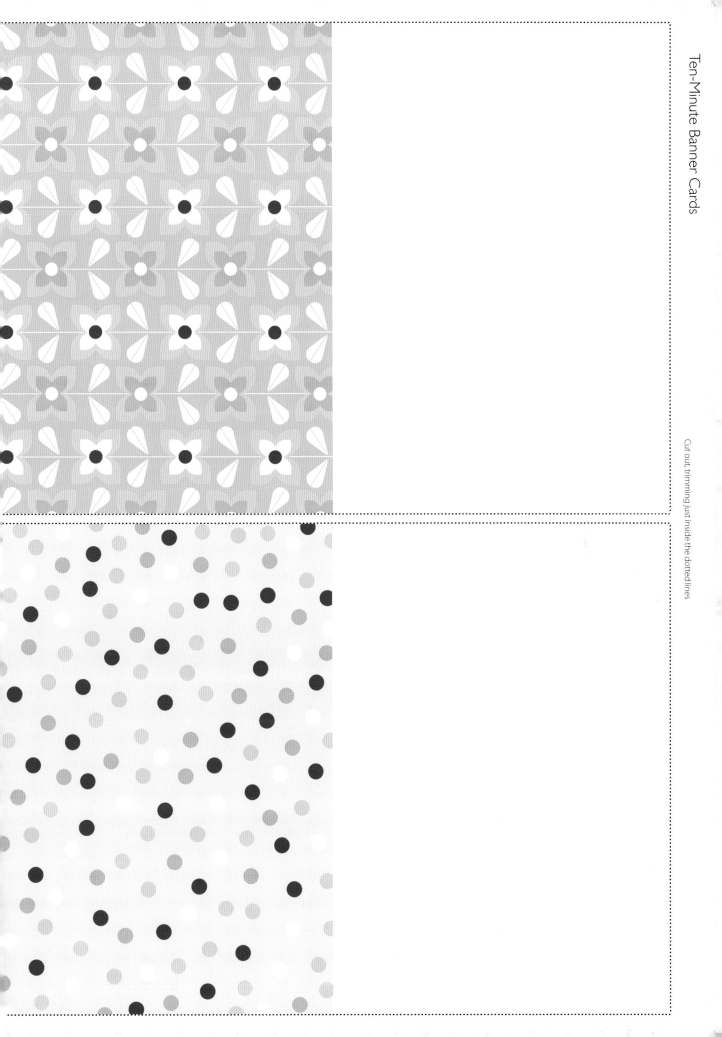

Cut out, trimming just inside the dotted lines

Posable Paper Dolls

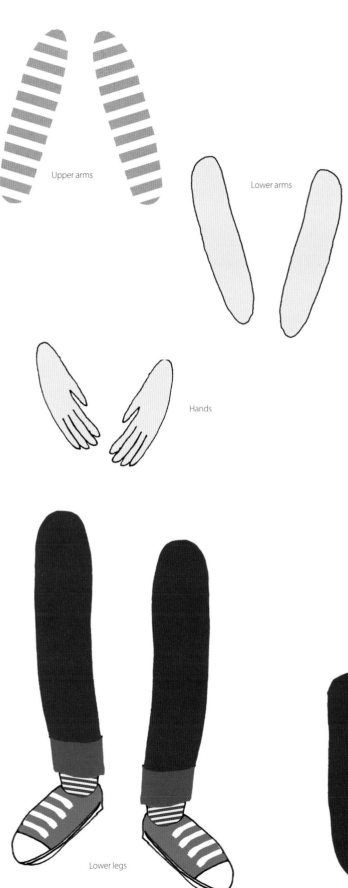

Upper arms

Lower arms

Hands

Lower legs

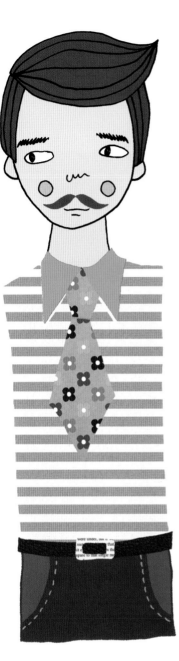

Upper legs

Lower arms

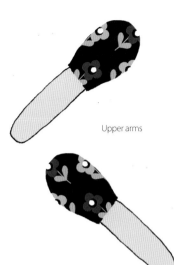

Upper arms

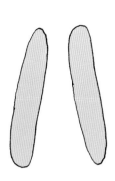

Hands

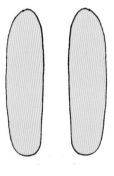

Upper legs

Lower legs

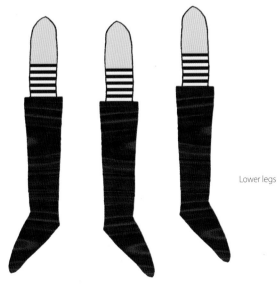

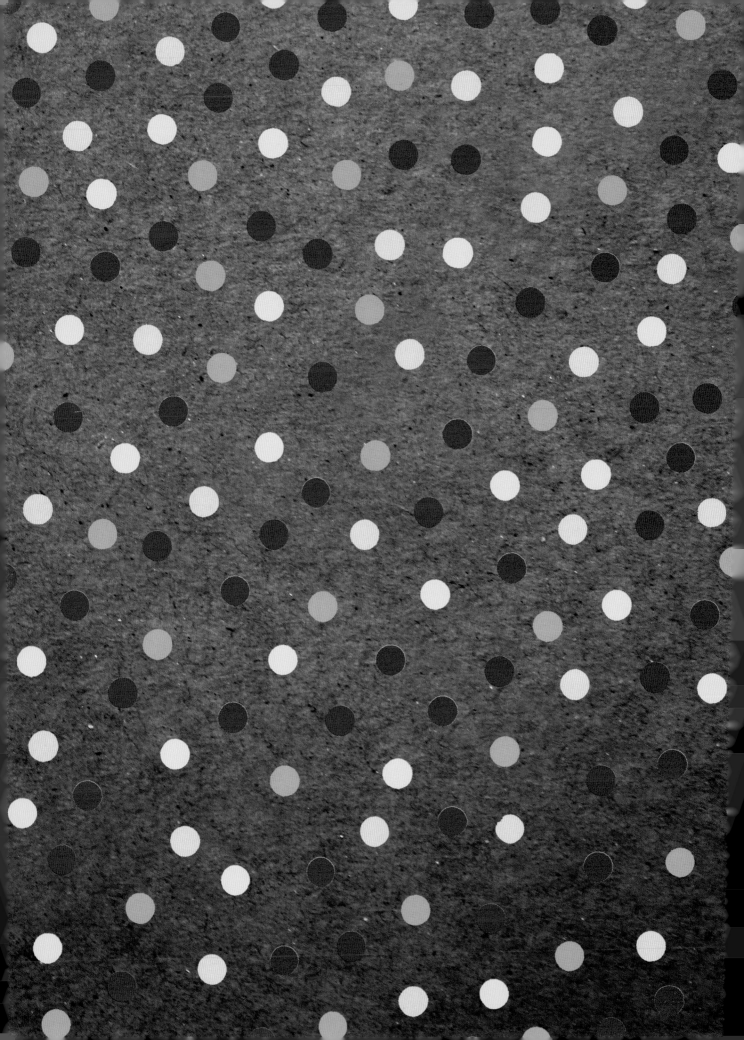

Alpine Mobile

ABOUT THE AUTHOR

Kirsty Neale is a freelance writer, illustrator and designer-maker living in London. She specializes in fabric and paper crafts, and enjoys combining new materials with vintage or repurposed finds. Her work has been published in numerous books and magazines, including *State of Craft* and *Mollie Makes*. She is a columnist for *Papercraft Inspirations* and writes a popular creative blog at www.kirstyneale.co.uk. Her first craft book, *Hoop-la! 100 Things To Do With Embroidery Hoops*, was published by David & Charles in 2013.

INDEX

A DAVID & CHARLES BOOK
© F&W Media International, Ltd 2014

David & Charles is an imprint of F&W Media International, Ltd
Brunel House, Forde Close, Newton Abbot, TQ12 4PU, UK

F&W Media International, Ltd is a subsidiary of F+W Media, Inc
10151 Carver Road, Suite #200, Blue Ash, OH 45242, USA

Text and Designs © Kirsty Neale
Layout and Photography © F&W Media International, Ltd 2014

First published in the UK and USA in 2014

A catalogue record for this book is available from the British Library.

ISBN-13: 978-1-4463-0427-3 paperback
ISBN-10: 1-4463-0427-2 paperback

Printed in China by RR Donnelley for:
F&W Media International, Ltd
Brunel House, Forde Close, Newton Abbot, TQ12 4PU, UK

10 9 8 7 6 5 4 3 2 1

Acquisitions Editor: Ame Verso
Desk Editor: Charlotte Andrew
Project Editor: Linda Clements
Art Editor: Jodie Lystor
Photographer: Jack Gorman
Senior Production Controller: Kelly Smith

F+W Media publishes high quality books on a wide range of subjects.
For more great book ideas visit: www.stitchcraftcreate.co.uk

ACKNOWLEDGMENTS

With thanks to all at D&C, including Ame, Jodie, Hannah, Lin and Charlotte, for your
enthusiasm, guidance and vision; to my family and friends for your love, patience
and all those times I had to put things off 'because of the book'; to my mum, who
taught me to make things, my dad, who taught me to love books and to Steve,
who showed me (almost) anything is possible.